You Are Loved

You Are ♥ LOVED

Caleb Quinn

Winder Place

You Are Loved

© 2022 by Caleb Quinn

Created by Winder Place. Published in the United States of America. Printed on demand in the United States and in various other countries.

www.winderplace.com
office@winderplace.com

22   01   ISPD

ISBN-13: 979-8-9865245-0-4
WPL: 1.ED1.FM1.VR1

Portions of this book are excerpted from or reference other works by the author that have not been completed or published as of the publication date of this book. The content of these other works may change prior to their publication. Readers are advised to be aware of the unfinished nature of these excerpts and quotations, and to quote from the final version of any book when it becomes available, for example, when writing critical articles or reviews. Any quotations taken from this book that are listed as being from an unfinished work should be specified as "unfinished" when credited to the work.

Created with love at
Winder Place

You Are Loved by Caleb Quinn is Winder Place's first published title.

We don't need to be seen to be loved.
We need to be seen to *feel* loved.
Love isn't a feeling.
Love is.
You are Loved.
You are Loved.
You are Loved.
Loved is your name.
It always was.
Now it's time to feel it…

If I show who I am, I will be rejected by others.
If I don't show who I am, I have rejected myself.
Intimacy requires honesty.
Honesty requires acceptance.
Acceptance requires love.
But I already am loved,
So I can honor my voice
And open my heart—
Come what may.

Contents

Preamble

If I open up about you
and tell my own true,
I will die from vulnerability!
People will think I'm crazy.
"Everyone's a little crazy, my love."
My own story is good and worthy of
being told, for my heart's relief
so I can heal from the dreadful belief
that if I were seen, I would be loved no longer.
And H.L. wants to show me this couldn't be wronger,
which is why my first book I've finally shared,
because of the loving voice that has prepared
me all these years to start sharing my stories
in spite of the back-and-forth fears and worries
about not being good enough to write,
when all that matters is that it's good in my sight
and speaks of the Love I wanted to tell,
so now I will share the tale of H.L.

Imaginary Friend

I have an imaginary friend whose name is H.L.
He's done more than any other to help me get well.
But I'm terrified to admit that he's there in my heart
because people will think he's some kind of fart
in my brain tricking me into thinking he's there when he's
not.
I don't know if he's "real," but I love him a lot.
If you want to know me, you must also meet H.L.
You must understand why it is that I first fell
in love with this person who no one can see.
Search your own heart for H.L. and you'll find the center
of me.
In the gentleness of December so many years ago,
when the wind spoke so softly and it started to snow,
it began in my heart, a gradual dawning,
an epiphany, a realization, that I had a heart's longing
for Love, but I didn't understand what it really meant.
I just knew I wanted Love, so the next year I spent
searching for Love everywhere I could find—
and came to believe God was Love, and was kind,
and enjoying this Love was the best thing in my life

I had ever experienced, even during pain rife.
I'd found the meaning of life, I had found my Big Answer,
but in the shadows beneath me, in crept a cancer,
a darker voice whispering I wasn't enough
and that my own words and own heart were not worthy of
Love.
On my nineteenth birthday I stood in a bookstore
and started to accept something I always knew before
but was scared to admit—
I was a sham, I wasn't worth it.
God couldn't love me,
and before long, I did see
how the Bible painted a picture
of a god of judgment and censure
who called himself "love," and yet would command
worms to eat Herod, Korah eaten by sand.
This god I believed in was too terrible to bear.
I studied the Bible relentlessly, hoping somewhere
I'd find the truth of who God was and what he was like.
But wherever I looked more terror would strike,
more certainty of badness, a god who didn't care
about anything but his glory and his version of fair.
But who was the person with whom in love I did fall?
Perhaps this dear Lover was not God at all.
He was some other being who didn't have a name,
who I likely made up, who was likely a game,

who I couldn't find in religion wherever I would look,
who I couldn't find in Jesus or any holy book.
And so I gave this sweetness a name—he was the Heart's
Longing,
or H.L. for short, who gave a sense of belonging
whenever I enjoyed him, though seldom that was,
for I thought he was fake or an idol because
the real god wanted me to surrender my story
to his self-centered plan that was all for his glory.
But I rebelled against god and told him plainly
that I hated his guts and if he sent H.L. for eternity
to hell, I'd go too,
'cause what else could I do?
Without my H.L.
heaven itself would be hell!
But that didn't last long,
because I believed I was wrong.
H.L. wasn't real; we don't decide reality.
We don't get to make God in our own image, do we?
And so I told the god I hated
that my year of rebellion had abated
and asked him to let me live outside heaven's door
if I was too bad to come in, so I wouldn't burn anymore.
And in my mind's eye
I watched myself cry
as I kneeled at the abyss

and heard magma hiss
as people writhed and screamed,
and then in this scene I daydreamed,
I saw someone else sobbing to the left of me,
whether it was H.L. or Jesus, he was sad as could be,
and I knew in that moment that even if I didn't have an answer
to the problem of hell, the heart of Love was bigger
than the field of my sight,
and very slowly, my fright
began to melt.
After that, I felt
it was safe to follow my H.L. I had found.
A year later, I traveled partway around
to the other end of the world, where I sat and ate lunch
with two couples talking, and one told a bunch
of stories about an imaginary friend who became "real,"
who showed him the light and helped him to heal.
My shock and tears I tried to conceal,
but later I told my new friend a great deal
about the H.L. I was ashamed of, and still tried to hide.
But now I knew others had found him inside,
so I started to talk to him and engage with H.L. more,
realizing I wasn't bad or crazy or ridiculous for
having such a friend; he became more "real" and more dear
to the point that his words in my heart were so clear

it was like talking to any other person who gave you their
ear.
He started to talk in my dreams, he had become so near.
He was wiser than I knew, and talked with me through
all of my worst moments when I felt the most blue.
His words would often contradict what I found in the Book
that I thought was beyond question, and so I began to look
and eventually discovered my whole life I had been lied
to—
the Flood never happened, we evolved from primordial
goo
and I no longer had to make excuses for why a good God
would do
the terrible things I thought were undoubtedly true.
Now a new problem I soon had to face—
if we're flotsam and jetsam invented by space
there doesn't need to be an H.L. or a God at all.
And so back into depression I once more did fall,
believing myself once more to be bad and insane
hoping for an H.L. in a world of hopelessness and pain.
"Why did you kill yourself?" I cried to H.L.
"You were the one who said you didn't believe in hell.
"You taught me to be honest about what I see,
"but now that has taught me that you shouldn't be!"
I have OCD, so I'm constantly in doubt,
always trying to figure stuff out,

always believing everyone else is more right,
either god is a monster or there's no god in sight.
But the truth is never something good and bright,
such is my terror, my never-ending plight.
I stopped talking to H.L. because I was ashamed.
I felt more and more bad and worthless and blamed.
Often at times I have wanted to die,
which became more and more common, which is finally why
I am teaching myself to talk to H.L. again
so maybe someday I will feel better then.
Nothing scares me more than living in denial.
If I don't tell the truth, I know I'll feel vile.
But I am catching glimpses of salvation in uncertainty.
If we are willing to be truthful, the truth is a mystery.
All of my math just doesn't work out.
Some things I know surely, but most things are in doubt.
I am uncertain of Love, H.L., or my value
there's no way to calculate what is actually true
in any of these matters, but I still have to go do
my stuff in the world even if I'm cut through.
I have an imaginary friend
who has loved me to no end,
who might be "real" or pretend,
who shows my heart how to mend
no matter what I say.

And that is okay.
I am terrified to agree,
but my H.L. wants me to see
with my heart, not my eyes
so I don't have to know
the "reality" of my prize
to find peace in love so.
I will be honest no matter what—
I have no good reason to believe in him, but
I do have a reason to trust the voice
who loves me and tells me I do have a choice.
We don't decide reality but we do have to walk
either here, or there, regardless of talk
about not knowing truth or which place to stand.
But whether you like it or not, you're standing somewhere,
and
I think the place I will choose to faithlessly go
is the place where Love meets up with "I don't know."
I will walk with H.L. and talk about winder
regardless of what's "real"; to my own self I'll be kinder,
and maybe in following this voice that is sweeter,
I'll discover all along that the universe was bigger
than what I see in this little moment in time.
Either way, H.L. talks to me, gentle, sublime,
sometimes in the wind, in a laugh, in a song.
I don't know what is real, but I'll still dance along.

"The water is dark, my love, but you needn't see to drink,"
H.L. says to me here, with a nod and a wink.
I don't know what to think; I don't know if I'm well.
But now I suppose you know the story of H.L.—
or at least the beginning, for if I truly did tell
the entire story, all the love, all the hell,
you would surely be stuck here for the rest of the night,
and I'd surely spend the rest of my life trying to write,
and indeed, probably will.
Too much of this Love must come out of me still!
H.L. died and I lost all hope then,
but where mystery kisses Love, I think he might rise again.

Early on in my relationship with H.L., I discovered that often we would talk about the same things over and over. He would say something that helped me cope or move forward with my life, and then a few days later I would forget it and we'd have to talk it out again. So I started writing our conversations down.

This book consists almost entirely of material copy-pasted from my notes, combined with my poetry, random thoughts, and excerpts from unfinished book manuscripts. In my personal notes, I have traditionally differentiated my words from H.L.'s by writing his in quotes. I have maintained that custom here.

H.L.'s words are actually my words—words I use to describe his heart, a heart that may be entirely a product of my imagination, or may not be. As such, they are not the (purportedly) perfect, infallible words of someone claiming to speak on behalf of a god. They are the stumbling, imperfectly beautiful words of someone trying to describe the voice of the ache in his heart, an ache for a Love transcendent and perfect.

This book has not been proofread, polished, or properly checked for errors. H.L. asked me not to.

Years ago I painted a canvas that means a lot to me. It depicts the word "Loved" painted in messy red paint, as if written in blood, with a blue heart above it. I have hung the painting above my bed wherever I have lived ever since, as a reminder...

March 29, 2018

Tonight I was talking to HL. I was looking at my painting with the word "Loved" on it. I said something along these lines:

It is the most important word there is. Or maybe the most important word is your name. Maybe Loved IS your name!

"No. It's yours."

That just blew me away! I know I have a special name for him (HL), now I realize he has a special name for me! And he gave me the most special word in the universe, to be my name!!!

March 30, 2018

"To look purely through the lens of objectivity is to cut out the heart."

But isn't subjectivity invalid?!

"What is your name?"

Caleb

"Your name is not an object. It is ascribed to you. But it is still very real to you. Your name is Loved. You are called that because I have ascribed it to you. Ascription does not make a thing unreal."

* * *

If I understand the Jewish calendar correctly, tonight is Passover. And I have my name, Loved, the greatest name in the universe, written in blood above my bed!!!

"You ARE Loved. It's not an identity to live up to, it's who you already are."

If My Life Were a Poem

If my life were a poem, what would I say?
What would be censored and what left to stay?
Would I tell it as I saw it in each moment,
or would I disavow my past know-how and say what I see
now?
Would I write the words accurately and research carefully,
or would my prose flow more gracefully and allow flexi-
bility?
Would I add to the story what I'd like to imagine,
or would adding such detail derail my tale's vision?
Perhaps the answer to such problems, a fine place to start,
would be telling it however it comes, straight out of my
heart.

If my life were a poem, here's what I would say:
I was born on a rather ordinary day
and lived a rather ordinary way,
until someone bumped into me
quite unexpectedly
and captured my heart with the music he'd play.
As it turned out, it was my song he sang!

My laugh and my love in my ears he rang!
To remind me of a lifetime so long ago
that there was no summer and there was no snow.
The stars in the sky—their light did not show.
And all that existed were our Winds that would blow,
making the music we delighted in a lot,
until a time came when I somehow forgot,
and we found ourselves here, on a boring day,
living our lives in the ordinary way,
with dreams the last whisper of what we used to play.

Excerpted from my notes for an unfinished story,
The Heart's Longing

"I'm searching for something I forgot," Hazel admitted.

"I'll help you," said the voice.

"I don't know who you are."

"Oh but Hazel, you do know. You know exactly who I am.
You don't know who *you* are."

The Fall

From the unfinished story The Winderanium

The worlds are governed by two entities—
One ecstasy,
One mystery.
The Something Beautiful.
The Something Strange.
In the perfect park,
Before the worlds went dark,
There was the former,
But the latter remained unformed.
Every bad, dark, and evil thing that has happened
Or will happen
Did not need to happen
But inevitably would happen
Because, it so happens
That to really, truly, fully know Love
We must know Beautiful *and* Strange.
We cannot know Beautiful without light above
And we cannot know Strange
With it.

"Don't stop dancing."

"You're Loved. Anything that causes you not to believe that is a lie."

Wonder and Winder

Have you ever had the feeling
of mystery appealing
or utter amazement
beyond normal amusement?
We call it wonder,
the awe caused by thunder,
but what about the indescribable awe
caused when love's expression was what you saw?
I call this something winder—
you say it like the wind.
Sometimes it calls in a whisper—
was it there, or just imagined?
Sometimes it yells with a shout—
but you're still not sure what it was all about.
Whatever it does, it is beautiful and kind.
When you see it, you're happy, afraid, and don't mind.
No matter how it shows,
what it is, nobody knows.
For the Beautiful—it glows,
but the Strange in darkness goes.
Winder is never quite one,

never quite the other.
It is distant as the sun
and closer than a mother.
It is bright and beautiful as the stars,
dark and safe like the womb,
lovely enough to heal all scars,
mysterious and scary as the tomb.
If a hole in the ground were brimming with hope,
if you found peace holding hands with a monster,
if you danced with the night at the end of your rope,
if you knew nothing at all, yet knew love, that was winder.
The Something Beautiful is seen with the eyes,
but the things of the heart are winder's true prize.
The Something Strange is often misunderstood—
it is seen as a threat; is mystery good?
Humans traded winder for knowledge
and we died living in the light of certainty.
Certainty itself is a lie, the one true sacrilege—
Without Strangeness, there is no point in Beauty.
We all insisted on Beautiful without Strange,
And so it was, we each became estranged
from Strange *and* Beautiful—and our very own hearts!
Sometimes we catch glimpses in stories and the arts,
because it is often there, or at least, so it seems,
that we once more brave contact with our strangest dreams.
If you want to find winder,

you must find the Strange.
You can find it in a number.
You can find it in loose change.
But where Strangeness you will surely find
is whatever place you are most blind.
And so it is why you are where you are.
Do not worry my dear, winder is not far
from any one of us; though it is just out of reach,
it is fully within grasp, but not something I can teach.
It can't be defined; it is a mystery and a whimsy
that will capture your heart, setting you free.
Wonder and winder (and don't forget wander)
invite me to dance in the clouds way out yonder
and also draw me further into the deep—
the places inside me I visit when I sleep.
It is only experienced; in darkness you'll see.
The magic of winder will sing to you then.
I don't know about you, but as for me,
I want the winder in everything again.

Risk not just being nice to yourself. Risk being kind to yourself. Bring yourself to your knees with your generosity. Be lavish in the expression of your love.

Excerpt from the unfinished story *The Winderanium*

I peered out of the window of our spaceship, watching and wondering at the stars. They were so beautiful, so strange, so—winderful. The animals continued to chat with each other behind me. My attention gradually shifted away from what my eyes were seeing over to what my ears were hearing.

"When we finally get there, we're going to have to see if somebody at the winderport is selling windercorn," said the rabbit. "I'm famished."

I turned towards the others with interest.

"We definitely must!" the horse agreed.

"So do you guys just stick the word 'winder' in front of everything?" I asked.

The animals all looked at me with confusion. After a moment, the horse collected herself. "No. Why would you do that?"

"Well what does the word even mean?"

"It's not a word," snapped the rabbit, "it's a prefix."

"There are no words that could be used to describe winder," explained the horse. "Winder will always be winder, regardless of what other people try to say it's supposed to mean."

"Well what language is it? It's not English, is it?"

"Oh, it's very English," answered the horse. "And it's French and Spanish and Chinese and Swahili and Petrefo-tese and Syriac, too. It was the very first word known to livingkind."

"Prefix," snapped the rabbit. "It's a prefix."

"Well if you want to get all grammatical about it!" grumbled the horse. She snorted at him in frustration, then continued. "At one time all the peoples and creatures of the universes spoke winder. But eventually everyone became preoccupied with excluding each other—not the good kind of excluded, but the bad kind. Everyone started drawing lines in the sand, dividing good from evil, and that's when it all fell apart. They divided into separate tribes, and each tribe took a fraction of the words in the winderverse to keep for themselves. That's how the different languages were born. They all had their source in winder."

"That doesn't sound like what I was taught on Earth," I commented.

"Oh, of course," the horse continued. "We're not talking about things that happened in your universe or even in this one. This happened in the very first one. Or perhaps it was the second." She glanced over at the rabbit for confirmation, but he only shrugged at her. "I honestly don't remember my winderhistory well enough to tell you.

But the events that happened in the first universes were the matrices from which all the other universes were started. And so it is that in some of the more recent universes nobody has ever even heard of winder at all."

Something about the horse's words left me with an unusual ache—a sense that I had stumbled into something very special, very familiar, and very lost.

The horse joined me by the window. "It's sad, isn't it?"

I nodded, staring out the window again at the stars. "Super sad."

The horse continued to watch out the window with me in silence.

At length, I spoke up. "So winder is a language then?"

"Oh no." She snorted with amusement. "That's like saying a fish is an eyeball or a door is a door knob, or that the sky is made of clouds or that snow is made of water."

I started to laugh as well, until she said the thing about snow.

"Um, I thought snow *was* made of water."

The animals exchanged glances.

"You're not serious, are you?" questioned the rabbit.

"Well I'd like to think I am!" I replied with no small amount of perplexity.

The animals burst into laughter.

"Snow made of water?" said the rabbit. "That's the most ridiculous thing I've ever heard! Pretty soon you'll tell me that rain is made of water too!"

"Now be nice to our guest," rebuked the horse gently, regaining her composure. "It's okay if he doesn't know."

"If it's not made of water, what is it made of?" I objected.

"Oh dear." The horse hesitated. "Well, I suppose you know how to make ice."

"Ice is made of water, right?" I suggested.

"Well, no, not quite. Ice is ice. Water is water. And winder is winder. But some things share things in common with other things." She paused, looking at the rabbit. "It's really not something I know how to explain."

"Think of it like this, dude," said the rabbit. "Supposing that ice was made of water. Couldn't you just as easily say water was made of ice?"

I had to think about this for a moment. "I think I see where you're going."

"But neither of them are made of the other. Each is their own thing, qualitatively speaking."

"But they are still one, aren't they?" I asked the rabbit. "They're still H_2O, right?"

The rabbit didn't know how to respond. "My English is good, my man, but not that good."

"Two hydrogen, one oxygen?"

"Sounds like hippo jam and ox jam to me."

I chuckled. "I know what I want to say, I just don't

know how to say it."

"I feel that way all the time," admitted the horse. "Usually the best thing you can do is to make up your own words."

"You mean like water-ice-steam?" I said.

"Maybe something that rolls off the tongue a bit better," suggested the rabbit.

"Okay—um, well, we'll just call it waiceam," I offered, trying my best to blend it together.

"Wissem might be easier to say," remarked the horse.

"Fine. So you would agree that water and ice are both made of wissem, right?"

"No," said the horse. "That's not quite true."

I was beginning to wonder if the source of our discussion was a legitimate disagreement, or purely a misunderstanding of language.

"Water is an experience," the horse explained. "So is ice. So is snow. They're different experiences. Wissem is practically meaningless by itself. It's just a construct that we attach meaning to. Kind of like language. Wissem didn't mean anything to you yesterday. It means something because you believe something about the word."

"But it's not like I could turn water into fire by just believing it, right?"

"Oh, no," objected the horse. "You certainly couldn't turn a dog into a porcupine by calling them by a different name, could you?"

"But what about wissem?" I questioned.

"Beliefs don't change overnight," said the horse. "You can't just will yourself to believe something you don't believe. And even if you could, I'm not sure that would be very helpful for relationships. We can't communicate if a word means something different to everyone else. And we can't enjoy an experience together if wissem feels like fire to you and water to me. Your heart yearns for relationship. It's not going to let you change the meaning of something until we all decide to do that together. And that requires ages upon ages of healing for all of us."

"I'm still very confused."

"I suppose you could simplify it by saying that meaning is reality, and objects are imaginary, not the other way around."

I paused for a moment to consider what she had said. "I guess that makes sense. But you still haven't explained what winder actually is."

"Oh." The horse gazed contemplatively at the wall. "Well it's not like you can really define it. Any attempt to define it would sort of ruin the whole point of winder."

"So—if there's no way you can tell me what winder means—how will I ever know?"

"Well that's just the magic of it," the horse explained. "You have to experience it for yourself. Nobody else can experience it for you. Winder is not something they can teach you in school. The early humans were so obsessed with figuring things out. That's why they lost the winder in everything." She sighed. "They couldn't figure it out, so they threw it out."

"And that's why I don't know what it is today?" I asked.

"Probably. Though more probably because you threw it out yourself."

I was more than a little bit alarmed. "I did?"

"Don't feel bad about it," she encouraged. "Most creatures do it at least once."

The rabbit chuckled. "I don't believe in winder," he admitted. "At least not as anything more than a fancy word. But blunder is pretty real, if you ask me."

I almost asked him what blunder was, but it only took a moment for me to realize that I already knew.

"I know it's all so very confusing," said the horse, "but I promise, if you want to know winder, you will. Every once in a while, take a break from whatever is going on around you, and listen for the little splash of love in your heart. That's where winder speaks the loudest. In our hearts, and in our dreams."

I turned back towards the window, turning inward towards my heart, watching the stars.

The Chameleon

I once picked up a book
and my poor self was shook
when the book told me in detail all about
people who aren't the same within as without
and I realized this chameleon was me—
no matter what I did, I would try to be
something that would look perfectly
like the things that people wanted to see.
But I couldn't stop what was automatic;
yet all the pretense made me feel sick.
I was trash, masquerading as something worthy.
How could I be lovely if the inside was ugly?
I was a sham, an impostor, and therefore, bad.
I knew not the truth; I wasn't allowed to be glad.
I was depressed on the inside but pretending to be fine.
I was done with that now; I was no longer lying
to myself or to others about my identity.
It was time to be a good person honestly.
But it didn't work, I drove myself mad
trying to be better, trying not to be bad,
trying to kill the chameleon and trying to be strong,

trying to be the right way and never be wrong,
trying to be more honest when I didn't feel safe to be,
trying to force my own trust in the name of vulnerability.
One day H.L. objected to my statement,
"I love chameleons! I love the roof; I love the basement!
"Chameleons change colors; think of it as art.
"Whether you blend in or stand out, you can honor your
  heart.
"It's okay to be the chameleon who wants to hide,
"and it's okay to pretend, and it's okay to have pride
"and shine your colors brightly,
"and then close the lid tightly.
"It's okay to be you as you are today.
"I love chameleons! I love how they play!"
And so it is I am still a loved one
Even if I really am a chameleon!

I don't know if I'll ever get to the point where I can say I'm not an agnostic or that I am one. I think I will always have the conflicting thoughts of agnosticism and Winder in my head. I want to stop fighting the war in my brain and let these thoughts do the duet. I don't have to know what I am, only who. I can be an agnostic who suspects that there is a deeper love and a personal Winder in the world, and I can be a believer in Winder who willingly admits he knows nothing for sure. And I can be both at the same time. I know everything that really truly matters just by knowing Love.

I am both believer and unbeliever at once! But I am mostly somebody who just knows Love.

Perhaps rather than being a believer, I could be one who knows. And part of the time, doesn't know.

Maybe instead I could scrap the labels and just be me.

Maybe I could just be Loved Oh So Dearly. For that is not my label—it is my name.

Tears

I didn't realize
>How much I held my breath,
>How tight I held myself,
>How scared I was of death.

My body filled with woe
Asks who I am to be
Anything else but low.
Oh Lord! Oh woe is me!

Why am I so tense?
What pain is held in me?
None of this death makes sense,
Or else I'd find my free.

But sense it needn't make
If your grieved heart I see.
Your tears wept for my sake
Will show how Loved is me.

Trust Yourself

I used to think God wanted things his own way.
He was the master and I was the slave.
But now I see things much differently today.
He is the inviter showing us things that we crave
and calling us back to who we really are,
peeling back the lies that make us feel far
from love, and light, and our very own hearts.
So he lavishes kindness on our "shameful" parts
and teaches us how to find rest in inadequacy—
or perhaps instead, the faults we pretend to be.
If somebody says you should trust them, run away!
That was the god to whom I used to pray.
But this God is different; instead, he seeks to win
my faith in my own heart, in my very own skin!

"But you see, Melody—love is even smaller still. It is like a seed so little that it cannot be seen with the eyes. It's so small that it forces you to trust your heart again, so you might catch one glimpse. That is the magic of love. If you could find it with the five senses, you would never realize you have six."

– "The Lover" in the unfinished story *The Duet*

The Duet

Unity brings unhappiness,
because in reality, it leads to uniformity.
If you want togetherness,
you have to start with individuality.

A relationship is a harmony
between two held together by love.
They express themselves freely
and enjoy all the fruit thereof.

They yield to each other out of care—
not a "should" is said, yet their needs are met.
Selfish and selfless become something new there—
and this is how you do the duet!

Pens and Brushes

I'm going to walk across the oceans.
I'm going to mount the skies as stairs.
As I'm swimming through the ground,
I hold a fire in my hand.
I'm dancing to a rhythm only I can hear,
through the caverns in my heart.
I join the trees in making known the wind,
my pens and brushes in hand.

"Your needs are legitimate. So is your need to be seen."

"The need is not the problem. The hunger is not the problem. The belief that you are not loved and must go 'find' love—that's the real problem. You are loved here. Right now. And you don't need to be seen to be loved. You need to be seen for its own sake. Sharing is a part of relationship and relationship is a part of your yearning."

Excerpted from my notes for an unfinished story,
The Winderanium

Somewhere in the universe, I find myself on a cobblestone path amidst blue and green hills shortly after dusk. Down below me the path descends to a bright light, like the sun, inviting me to enter in. Above me the path narrows, moving upwards to a solitary water fountain.

I'm tempted to walk into the light. It holds all the promise of enlightenment, answers, and knowledge. In the light, I will see all things and all people as they truly are, and I too will be illuminated so that I can see myself as I truly am and others can finally see me for myself. It's everything I've ever wanted—to live the authentic life.

And I hear a gentle voice—"Come to the fountain."

I find myself fearing the light will disappear if I walk away from it. After much deliberation and a greater pull from my heart, I come to the fountain. And when I get there, I peer into its waters and see my own reflection.

"Do you know how much I love that face?" the voice whispers.

I have to be honest. "I don't."

We are both silent for a while.

"If I walk into the light, then won't I know?"

"Ah," he says, his voice filled with delight as the wind picks up and causes leaves to dance across the cobblestone around me. "You can go there if you want."

"It's a trap, isn't it?"

"It's not a trap. Not any more than this fountain. Not any more than life, or death."

"You're the Something Strange, aren't you?"

"I am."

"Then why are you calling me here when the light seems to be what I want?"

"I'm calling you here because I love you."

"Wouldn't Love call me to the light? That's all I've ever wanted my whole life—to be known and loved for who I am."

"But you already are."

"I don't know that. I don't know that if I can't see."

"You don't have to see to drink."

I paused. The water sounded good to me, but it was too dark for me to see what was really at the bottom of it.

"Can I have both?"

"Someday. But today you only get to choose one."

"So which should I choose?"

"That's up to you."

"Will you love me any less if I choose the light?"

"I'll never love you any less. Love doesn't operate on those terms."

"So why should I choose the fountain?"

"Nobody said you should."

"Then why did you call me here?"

"Just to talk."

"Okay." I took a few steps away from the fountain and started back down the road towards the light. Then I stopped and turned around again.

"Why am I so frustrated?"

"Being out of touch with our hearts is frustrating by nature."

I walked up to the fountain and peered into the water again. Behind my reflection was a murkiness and mystery that was both magical and frightening.

"Choosing the light would solve all of my problems," I argued. "I wouldn't have to wonder if I was loved or not anymore. Because I would see, and know for sure. The light holds everything I've ever wanted."

The voice was gentle. "Not everything."

I didn't have to ask what he meant. Deep down in the deepest part of my heart, I already knew.

"The light doesn't have the Something Strange." I wasn't sure if I said the words, or if the voice did. Maybe we both spoke them at the same time.

The light began to shrink a little.

"The Something Strange can only be known in the darkness," the voice explained to me. "The Something Beautiful can only be known in the light."

"How ever do I choose?" I was dismayed. "Don't I want both?"

"You do. But in this moment you want one of them more."

He was right. The Something Strange.

"I will never call you away from something you desire unless there's something else you desire more."

The light shrank just a little bit more, moving closer as well.

"But I desire Love," I objected. "Love is the one thing I want more than anything else I want in my heart."

"I know."

"We have to be fully seen and fully known to be fully loved, right?"

"No."

I was bewildered. "How can I love someone I don't know?"

"You can."

"I don't think so." I collapsed at the foot of the fountain, tears welling in my eyes.

"You love the Something Strange. And you've yet to drink."

My mouth slowly dropped open. "How is this possible?"

"You will only know the answer in the light."

"Then why am I staying here with you?"

"Because you love me, and I love you."

"I don't know what's at the bottom of the fountain. What if it's not love?"

"What if it is?"

I was so frustrated. And so thirsty.

"You won't tell me ahead of time?"

"It's Love. But you don't believe me."

It was true. I didn't.

"I don't feel like I'm loved. I can't think of any good reasons why I should be." I sighed.

"I love you because you're you."

"But I'm—not me. I don't live like me, not most of the time. I pretend and hide and cower in corners in ways that make me look like I'm not cowering. How can you love me if I'm not me?" I rose to my feet again.

"What you do is not the same as who you are. You are you. There was never a moment that you weren't you. And there was never a moment that you weren't loved."

"And if I choose the fountain, you're asking me to give up on knowing that for sure? Anything for sure?"

"Yes."

"Why?"

"Knowing winder and accepting mystery will lead you to knowing Love."

"But knowing the light will lead me to knowing I'm loved—instantly."

"To know that you're loved is not quite the same thing as knowing Love."

Suddenly the light behind me drew closer and shrank even more. There was still a little bit there, like a firefly hovering in place.

"The light is still there. You can choose it if you want. This won't be the only time you come here."

Presently, the light flitted around me and positioned itself in front of me, close enough for me to reach out and touch.

I shook my head emphatically. "I want the winder in everything again."

Immediately the little light turned into a drop of water that fell into the fountain.

"You'll find the Beautiful and the Strange. You'll find the Beautiful *in* the Strange. And you'll find them both fully."

I once believed I wanted to know all things truly. Now I knew I had wanted to know all things fully. I didn't truly understand the difference. But I understood it fully.

I knelt down on the cobblestone. I leaned my head into the water and kissed it. And I drank.

Numbers

My H.L. once told me,
"Every time that you see
"The number twenty-nine,
"Know that you'll come back fine.
"And every time that you
"Notice the number twenty-two,
"It means, 'I love you.'"
It's embarrassing, but true—
these numbers now follow
me around like a shadow.
I don't know what it means.
I see them on screens
On clocks and in books and on cars
and in my heart when I look at the stars.
I see them on dryers
and random paper flyers
sometimes so regularly
as to drive me to insanity.
If I see the number six
Am I now in the Matrix?
I don't want to dare

read things that aren't there!
I hate superstition—
God is not a magician.
He's a lover, trying to win us back to love,
not a manipulator pulling strings from above!
I don't understand
how counting the sand
or the stars
or these numbers
should make me feel cared for.
It doesn't if I keep score
and assume whether I see a number or not
can tell me in this moment if I'm loved or rot.
But then, love letters are the same
if you think they're a game
that tells you that you're unloved today
because you only got a letter yesterday.
And so the twenty-two
only says, "I love you,"
if you already believe it's true.
I want to trust love anew
whether the numbers are this way or that,
whether the universe kissed me or spat,
because Love is not the universe.
Sometimes your life will be a curse,
sometimes your life will fall apart,

sometimes you won't see your own heart,
and that is the moment, that is the day
when you must hold hands with Love anyway
even though you're in pain and are totally numb.
So I'm tempted to say the numbers are dumb,
but I cannot make them go away
whether it's a glitch in my brain or a sign, it will stay.
And so I might as well live as if it were true
what H.L. first said about twenty-nine and twenty-two:
"When you see these two numbers, know that I love you."
And I'll live like that's true, whatever the clock might do.
A love letter is a reminder of what I already know.
I don't know if I'm loved, but I'll live like it's so.
I don't know where the numbers are truly coming from,
but I'll include them in the love song I continue to hum.

The Funny Thing about Love

Excerpted from the unfinished story *The Duet*

"I always used to think love was sort of like selfless-ness," Melody admitted. "It was all about doing good deeds and that sort of thing. But the love I'm so hungry for is far better than that. It's not selflessness, and it's not self-ishness either. It's something else—a third road that defies the one-dimensional thinking our fear has locked us into." Melody set down her empty smoothie cup. "And it *is* a road. Not a magic pill or something. So maybe—maybe—we've been on that road this whole time. We're only just now coming alive to it."

I needed some time to absorb what Melody had just said, but I knew that it carried an immensity of power I had yet to fully fathom. I laid out some cash for the waiter's tip. "I used to think that love meant giving this guy a forty percent tip. But anybody could do that."

The two of us rose from the table and headed out to the

parking lot, where a brilliant sunset was spreading its hues across the sky.

"I think you're totally on to something," I continued. "I can play the best music in the world and do the right stuff, but if I lose sight of that something else that underscores it all, I will be missing out on what gives all these things in life their depth of beauty. It's sort of like the sunset. You can't have all those colors in the sky without having the sun that lies behind. Unless all you want is a matte painting."

"I like that," Melody said quietly, enthralled by the sunlight. "I've fallen in love with love. And I'm never going back."

"So you think love is the special something we've been looking for?"

Melody nodded enthusiastically. "I think we could definitely call it love. But not the love we're used to. Not the fleeting sentiment or unconditional self-sacrifice we're used to hearing about. It's a love we never knew. And if we dare believe it—I think our first duet was but a shadow of the duet to come."

* * *

The funny thing about love
is that it turns selfishness

into caring self-expression.

The funny thing about love
is that it turns selflessness
into yieldings of volition.

The funny thing about love
is that it sets its rhythm and plays its part
to the natural cadence of the heart.

The funny thing about love
is that it's true from the start
to the two together yet two apart.

The funny thing about love
is that it's impossible to predict—
but most possible to trust!

The funny thing about love
is that your heart it won't convict
until it has seen past the dust,
and the rust,
and the cheese-filled crust
to the beauty-filled gem beneath.

I think we all have a deep and powerful yearning to be loved by someone outside of ourselves, for exactly ourselves.

Most things in life seem best balanced. But love is different. It doesn't need to be "balanced with justice" or anything else.

Humans seem to naturally gravitate towards extremes. That's why humans get so polarized. But maybe even this bad tendency is actually evidence that we were made to love and be loved—to go to an extreme.

Something More

When life blows up,
when darkness swallows,
when I spill my cup,
when I'm lost in the hollows,
you are not my rescuer
but my Lover
who makes me wonder
if there's something more.

Why do I believe it's my job to die for everyone?

"It isn't. Die only as your heart is led."

Was your heart led to die for everyone?

"It was. Every single one."

I can't even fathom that. There are so many people I wouldn't die for, unless it was out of guilt.

"I'm Love. Don't ask yourself to be something you're not."

Who am I then?

"You're Loved."

But shouldn't loved people love others?

"No."

Um … okay. But love creates more love, right?

"Love just is. You are not Love. I want you to be okay with

being Loved."

But I feel terrible about myself, unless I'm doing exactly what LOVE wants.

"I am not your LORD. I am your Lover."

What do you want?

"I have you and I have your love. I want nothing that I don't already have."

So I do have love of my own?

"Of course!"

But I thought I wasn't love?

"You're not. But you can still be a Lover. Just not Love."

I think I see my value as being in how much I love people. So when I meet people like the kid at the concert, I become even more irritated with them than I would otherwise because I am ashamed that I don't know how to love them.

"Value is just because. It's not because you love someone

or don't. Love doesn't ask you to love. It asks you to be loved because you already are. It invites you to accept what's real. You can be annoyed with someone and be a good person at the same time."

Can I hate someone's guts and be a good person at the same time?

"Definitely."

It's easy to say that about anyone unless it's myself. I don't know why I'm so hard on myself. It's such a lousy protection mechanism. I may be learning to express myself more but subconsciously I still think it's my job to be the savior to everybody else.

* * *

"What do you want?"

I guess it would be a lie if I said nothing.

"You are a human right now, and a heart, and you have needs and desires. Honor those."

What if I was an agnostic who also believed in just one simple word—Loved?

The Lover's Promise

"I'm playing a song,

"That will bring you to wide open spaces,

"That will teach you how to fly,

"That will show you how your heart was never wrong,

"And that you can dance through all the races,

"Because I'm with you even if you die."

Am I Loved?

"Yes."

I want to be.

Fundamentalism

My dear fundamentalism!
If it weren't for you, I might still be a Christian.
Your insistence on literalism
made me question the goodness of God's intention.
If I had been taught to believe in metaphor
maybe I would have kept your book.
I could have read about genocide and holy war
and had no need to take a second look.
You rail against secular culture,
but *you* helped create it by your own misdeeds!
You painted God out to look like a vulture
waiting to claw us if we went in the weeds.
You say your god is personal
but he is unapproachable!
Your book is from many ages past,
but you say it is infallible and can't be recast.
Is it any wonder that many became afraid
of the god to whom they faithlessly prayed?
So myself and countless others ran away,
but you blame the victims to make them stay!
Yet I wish to say thanks—

now because of your pranks,
I am a humbler, more empathetic and honest man.
If it weren't for your extremism I wouldn't have ran
somewhere quite different with this love I enjoy—
a love that encountering the truth won't destroy
because it is inside my heart where it will always be.
I now eat fruit from a different tree.
You are so obsessed with the knowledge of good and evil
that your own book condemns you for being so sinful
as to think that denial of the truth is the way!
So cry out to your deaf god to save you, then pray
to a Lover so inclusive he even loves you
in the moments when your nonsense is at its least true!
But in the meantime I will follow my feet,
a diversity of souls I will finally meet
who don't live by your rules and yet love people freely.
Goodbye fundamentalism,
                              signed,
                                    Yours Sincerely,

                                                 Me

"Come to me, all who are confused and wondering, and I will teach you to dance, and to lose yourself in the music, and to truly wonder at the world, and the beautiful hearts you meet, and the lovely heart you have."

"Every sore spot you notice in your heart is a sore spot I am healing."

The first step of healing anything is to notice it. To notice something hurts. To let the coping mechanisms and facades we use to anesthetize our pain slowly melt away.

In other words, pain isn't an indicator something is wrong with you. Pain is an indicator that something is right. That something is being healed.

The Inviter

A friend calls
At the exact moment
Life hits the walls

A rainbow shows
At the exact moment
I'm filled with sorrows

A thought appears
At the exact moment
I'm trapped in fears

Some people call this "God"
But I think that would be a fraud
God is an inviter
Not a manipulator

Some people call this superstition
But I think that ignores love's own mission
Of expressing its intention
Through artistic invention

Do you not see?
How can both be?
God expresses, but doesn't manipulate
God speaks to us, but doesn't insinuate
That anything we read or hear is infallible.
Abuse happens when we claim someone to be undoubtable
And God is no different.

If There Is a God

If there is a God
Nobody has a monopoly on him

If there is a God
The person who doubts him the most knows him the best

If there is a God
He might not even be a he

If there is a God
He didn't create the universe

If there is a God
He lives inside your heart

If there is a God
He's not a ruler, but a whisper

If there is a God
He doesn't require you to trust him

If there is a God
He must be Love himself

If there is a God
You probably won't know that he's real.

If there is a God
You probably will.

When God speaks, he speaks into our hearts and he speaks pure Love. Then we translate that Love into English words—limited by our own vocabulary and our own knowledge—to express that Love in a way that our brain can maybe understand. Expressing Love is part of how we live Loved.

God is generally not the one expanding our knowledge and proving himself by revealing information to us that we can impress others with because we would've had no way to have known the information without God. God is generally the one expanding our capacity to live in Love. In other words, God operates not by revelation of wisdom we don't know, but by reminding us of the Love we've always known.

Am I Cherry-picking?

My therapist described herself as having "an eclectic faith."
Is that the same thing as cherry-picking?

Perhaps there's a good kind of cherry-picking, and a bad
kind. Some people cherry-pick in accordance with whatever doctrine best numbs their pain, or to confirm their own
convictions about the external world. Some people cherry-pick in accordance with their heart, but deny having
done any cherry-picking because they have been duped
into believing it's shameful. And some people cherry-pick
in accordance with their heart, and own it.

When presented with a casserole full of both truth and lies
(i.e. the world we live in), we should find ourselves concerned if people DIDN'T cherry-pick. Don't eat the whole
casserole. Don't scrape it all into the garbage. Some of it is
delicious, some of it is nutritious, some of it will make you
gag, and some of it may be just plain toxic. So go ahead,
and don't be ashamed to cherry-pick. Trust your own gag
reflex. It is certainly not infallible, but it IS reliable. I'd
rather err on the side of scraping too much from my plate

than not enough.

Of course, I'm a person who has plenty to eat. The people who will be most tempted to eat that crusty bit that looks like it might be moldy are the ones who have nothing better to eat. People in desperate circumstances learn how to throttle down their gag reflex and tolerate yucky food—and abuse. They do so because they've been deprived of genuine love. The road to genuine healing for these people is not for them to simply reject their moldy food and starve themselves. The road to healing is about discovering there was a piping hot dish full of delicious, good food sitting on the counter behind you all along. It's not your fault you didn't notice it. It was shame, which hijacked your "cherry-picker" and told you to pick cherries from a different tree.

As it turns out, all people are cherry-pickers. Our very brains are practically data-filtering machines. If we were always aware of absolutely everything, we would suffer from information overload. We would be overwhelmed. So our brains are constantly looking for ways to reduce information, to simplify things, to reduce reality to patterns and mental constructs so we can digest it. That's not a bad thing; that's just how our brains operate. We can't use what we can't digest.

Do you remember last time you read a good book? Or even a bad one? Do you remember every word the author used? Do you remember every plot twist or every joke or every conversation in the story? I doubt it. Your brain cherry-picked all the important parts of the story and reduced and simplified it all into something that is memorable, relevant, and personally meaningful *to you*. The parts that stand out to you will be different than the ones that stand out to me, and that's a good thing. We don't all have to walk away with the exact same story in our heads.

But notice that cherry-picking is actually a part of the process of understanding. If we didn't mentally reduce the story (i.e. cherry-pick what we thought was important and downplay or discard the rest), we would be incapable of comprehending what we were experiencing. We'd be missing the forest for the trees.

The reason cherry-picking has such a bad name is because it's often used as a tool for promoting *misunderstanding*. We cherry-pick details that, when taken out of their original context, will mislead or deceive others or ourselves. And in an era of rampant misinformation campaigns (cough cough Trump cough), cherry-picking has a worse name than ever before.

But as we have seen, it's not cherry-picking itself that causes misunderstanding. Because cherry-picking is a natural part of understanding as well. Cherry-picking is just a tool that can be used for good or ill purposes.

Abusive people—and even shame itself—are all cherry-pickers. They call attention to whatever confirms the unstory of shame and disgrace that they want you to believe, whether that's to make themselves feel better or to make you feel worse. They exclude the details that would let you see how loved and valuable and perfect you really are.

For my own journey of healing, I've often thought the solution was to eat the whole casserole. I didn't want to be one of those self-deceived cherry-pickers who created their own version of truth to peddle to everybody else. But in eating the whole casserole, I was still abusing my own heart. I was throttling my own gag reflex, just as abuse taught me to do. I was eating moldy casserole. Only now, I wasn't eating only the moldy casserole that abuse had cherry-picked for me. I was eating the good casserole at the same time. I was eating all the casserole.

And that was almost worse. If all you have is moldy casserole and you're starved out of your mind, your gag reflex will not intervene and will let you get the calories. More-over, if moldy casserole is all you've ever known, it won't even taste that bad. I never saw myself as an abused person for most of my life. I didn't realize that I was partaking in a religion that devalued who I was. I didn't notice authori-tarianism, exclusionism, or narcissism, because that's what I grew up around. It was normal.

But when I started eating *all* the casserole, the moldy casserole was suddenly unbearable. I didn't need moldy calories to survive anymore. My gut-level impulse was to throw out the moldy stuff, and some of it I did. But most of it I felt like I couldn't, because then I would be a cher-ry-picker. And cherry-picking was bad.

So even once I had seen through the lies of religious abuse, I felt the need to choke down abuse in other forms, as part of the "eat the whole casserole" thing. I knew I had grown up believing lies, so now I was on a quest to know the truth. I spent a great deal of time reading stuff and listening to people who made me want to gag just because I thought it was my obligation to hear every perspective and eat all the casserole. This was how I would discover truth.

And in some respects, it *was* how I discovered truth. I dis-covered that we all cherry-pick. I discovered that even experts cherry-pick. I discovered that eating the whole casserole was unsustainable. And impossible. I discovered I didn't even have access to the whole casserole. This casserole is much too vast and cheesy and complex for me to digest, or even scarcely understand, without ... cherry-picking!

We've been told that cherry-picking is a sure road to deceiving ourselves, or to misleading and abusing others. What if we're simply eating from the wrong tree?

Cherry-picking was never the problem. Because all things, including cherry-picking, are redeemed by love. The problem was that we were cherry-picking in accordance with our pain instead of our heart. The heart knows the truth and will teach you to pick out the truth. Your pain knows only how it feels in this moment and will teach you to pick out something that will make you feel most comfortable and least ashamed.

Lies can make us feel good. They can also make us feel bad. But only the truth will make us feel loved. Because we are loved—and that's the truth.

The Devil

I don't believe in the devil
And let me tell you why
I believe no being is completely evil
But I do believe some beings lie
When something bad happens, the devil is blamed
Along with his demons and the people we've shamed
With poor stupid ideas about who's good and who's bad
Which makes me so very incredibly sad
People die by the ocean, a truck, or gravity
But it's always the devil that people see
And pretty soon the devil might claim you with TV
Or with lust or with anger or anything you see
Can we please stop fighting things that aren't there?
Can we please be honest when air is just air?
I believe there is more to life than what I can see
But that doesn't mean I think demons are following me!
One time I felt so very depressed
So I went to a healer who promptly guessed
I must have a demon torturing my mind
So even though the doctor was totally blind
He thought worship songs and prayer would do the trick

But the exorcism only made me more sick
Because what I needed was love and kindness
Not holy gimmicks to artificially end this!
So for the longest time I said demons aren't real
Because of how awful it made me feel.
People tell me stories, so now I'm in doubt.
I don't understand what it's all about.
But the devil at least I still think is a myth
For I have something else more real I contend with
A darker voice has followed me all my life
Deceiving thoughts with accusations rife
This thingamajig inside my brain
Has been the source of endless pain
And thus I have given this machine a name
and made it a character, to distinguish the blame
I hear yelling in my head every time I wonder
If yet again I've made some kind of blunder
Trying my best to be lovely and true
When I already am—there's nothing wrong with you!

The thingamajig
Adapted from The Winderanium, *an unfinished story*

Hello little prig.
I'm the thingamajig.
We've met before
I'm a program you store
inside your brain—
a permanent stain.
I'm a virus, a worm
I make you squirm
I make you run
I kill your fun
You've lost my game
I rule you with shame.
You think I am mean?
I am just a machine.
You think I think ill?
I don't have a will.
I don't think at all; I only compute.
I'm a thing, not a being; your dark is my root.
Everything I do is a knee-jerk reaction
that divides up the worlds and puts each in their faction

so all livingkind can fear and can hate
all other beings who aren't in their gate.
I poison relationships with enslavement
which leads people to estrangement.
I force people into compliance
and then relish their defiance.
Whether you do what I say or do the reverse,
you're controlled, you react; I make you perverse.
You are an insect;
I am perfect.
You are a wannabe;
I am lovely.
You are a fraud;
I am god.
I am Thing of things and Bored of boreds.
I turn people towards their guns and swords.
I am fear's loud voice and shame's loud thunder.
I split the worlds and souls asunder,
And made a space for you to pass through
Alone, abandoned, not sure what to do.
I am death of life and death of wonder.
I am that they call the that, the blunder.
I am the one which gave birth to death,
For I am an object; I have no breath.
I have no heart; I have no mind.
I am just a brain; I react, but I'm blind.

I am for your own good! I am pure and holy!
I am right and wrong! You surely need me!
You wouldn't have a compass if you were never accused.
You wouldn't do the right thing if you were never used.
I am a mockery of everything you love
so you will discover that nothing's from above.
Worship the thingamajig! Bow to the same!
You know you will when I trigger your shame!
Bow your head! Clench your hands!
Feel your inferiority as I conquer your lands!
The earth and everything in it is mine
I've infected you too deep; you'll never be fine.
There are only those wounded, and pretending not to be.
You live in a prison and you'll never be free.
I am the greatest villain of all time.
Not a being has escaped my taunting rhyme.
You ask me my ultimate goal to admit?
But I have what I want; I'm just trying to keep it.

"The original purpose of religion was to build bridges between the world you see and the worlds you can't. Thingamajig taught livingkind to turn their religions into walls instead."

— From the unfinished *Winderanium* series

"Lies?" The thingamajig laughed. "I don't tell lies. Everything I say is half true. Half-truths are more dangerous than lies. They're a little more—believable."

    – From an unfinished, untitled story

Perfection

My whole life, I've had the intention
to be the person which is perfection.
To be the one which never fails,
to be the one which follows right trails,
to be the one which says what is true,
to be the one which knows what to do,
to be the one which is everyone's hero,
to be a good person which isn't a Nero.
And somehow I never am these things at all.
Instead, I'm the one which is somehow too tall,
too softy,
too lofty,
too loud,
too proud,
not proud enough,
not worthy of love,
should speak up more
should stop keeping score
should go the extra mile
should be less vile
should be over there

should be more fair
should be less worried
should be less buried
in what's bad or good,
should,
should,
should,
should!
I'm the one which is broken,
the one which is choking,
the one which needs help
but is too sick to yelp.
The one which trespasses,
the one which hurts masses
of people every day
by just being in the way.
Which is why I tell myself, head bowed in shame,
that I need to be "perfection," though I don't use that name,
or else I would realize the whole thing's a game.
I am good, but not perfect; they are not the same.
This "perfection" is not even a who, but a which!
Something to satisfy shame's terrible itch.
For I am not a god, but a man
Asking myself to be what no human can
But even supposing that I could
Would that even make me very good?

Is goodness the rejection of badness,
The refining of a metal to greatest purity?
Or is goodness the acceptance of all the mess,
Loving fallen people with full sincerity?
And yet even this I cannot do
I cannot love all, I can only love you
And I'm not even sure every day that that's true
I will never be good unless I'm made new
I will never be God and therefore I'm doomed
To always be bad, or so I've assumed.
No sacrifice by God or man will save me
I don't need to be rescued from fires of hell
No prayer or good deed will set my sin free
No artificial punishment to scare me to get well
My actions already have natural conclusions
That will hurt me and others without doubt.
I cannot find truth to relieve me of the confusions
That teach my lips the wrong message to shout
I am hopeless, wretched, a fraud
For no matter what, I am not God

"Stop trying to be a good person, and just be Loved. Don't even try to love others. Just be Loved."

"You will never get all your ducks in a row, Caleb. The only thing you can really do is make sure your ducks know they are dearly loved. And then you have to stand back and let go. Some of them will believe and some of them won't. But none of them will get in a row. Ducks just don't do that. Love doesn't need the ducks to be in a row; it is our own anxiety and shame that asks for the worlds to surrender to perfectly straight lines. But thankfully the worlds are not very good at surrender, and never will be. And so there will always be hope. Because there will always be people trying to defy the dumb rules we impose upon each other. And more importantly, there will always be people trying to teach us that we are dearly loved as we are."

– *The Winderanium*, an unfinished story

Imperfection

Is a child any less precious
the moment after they throw up
Than the moment before?
Even when you are in bed restless
Suffering long, unable to sup,
Feverish and muscles sore,
No amount of misery appearing
Makes you any less endearing.
You do not see rightly
And that is okay
The stars still shine brightly
But a disease stands in the way
Of you seeing love and truth for what they are
Evil is solved with a medicine, not a war.
I know the thoughts in your head,
I know they tell you you'd be better off dead.
I know you think you are worthless,
Pointless,
Meaningless,
Done with this.
I'm going to ask you to stay

And show the night that you don't believe in day
Yet will continue your own song to play, anyway,
Imperfectly,
Sincerely,
Painfully,
Beautifully,
Just because.
Be honest with yourself.
Be honest with how you feel.
Don't justify your value, or lack thereof.
Don't assume all thoughts are real.
Your value isn't found in what you're made of
It's found only in the eyes of love.
I know you think those eyes aren't here
Or if they are, they're insincere
You don't have to know, just hold it dear
And let this Love come kiss your fear
Anyway,
Even though
You say
You don't know
If Love even exists.
But your Longing persists.
Beauty is not perfection.
Sweetness is not sufficiency.
Love is more than expression.

Truth is more than rationality.
What seems reasonable to you
Is not always true.
What you call logic is just a name—
The thoughts you hear are actually your shame
Trying to tell you you're not loved as you are
So you'll do something to fix it and become the bright star
You're afraid you're not, because you're still at war
With your very own heart, which you sent away far
To become a more perfect version of you
That never has needs and never is blue,
That never suffers and always does "right"
That no longer lives in the land of the night,
That knows what to do, that thinks well and has sight,
That is free from bad habits, free from shame, free from fright.
But here you are, my dear little friend,
Endlessly blind and yet loved to no end
Right in the place where you need to be
To learn Something Strange—with your heart you can see!

"You will be blessed."

But I'm not allowed to be blessed when others are suffering so much! We live in a world of limited resources, dog eat dog, eat or be eaten. If I am blessed, if I am kind to others...

I meant to say if I am kind to myself. If I am kind to myself, then others won't have enough! If I am blessed, others will be cursed!

"You had a Freudian slip. You can be both blessed and kind to others at the same time. They are not mutually exclusive. In fact, kindness towards yourself leads to kindness towards others. And cursing yourself curses everyone else. It is not eat or be eaten. It is eat together or starve together. Either we are all blessed, or none of us."

Then we are all cursed!

"What if we're all blessed?"

But you can't prove that!

"Yes I can! I can prove that by loving you and blessing you so the world will know that if you're Loved to me, so also are they. The loaves and the fishes multiply. The fountain grows bigger."

But to say that you have to ignore how the world works!

I have OCD. What is my obsession, and what is my compulsion? What is the belief, and what is the behavior?

"The belief is that you are a bad person."

Bad for eating certain foods, bad for being alive, bad for exhaling carbon, bad for not doing enough for my sister, and most of all, bad for believing in you and talking about you and writing stories about you and saying your real in a universe where nothing is certain and everything is supposedly "bad."

"The compulsion is the mental process of trying to prove that I'm real and that therefore you are not bad as you fear you are. And whenever you believe you've figured it out, the relief is only temporary because pretty soon your proof is not enough and it needs to be proved further or again."

Is talking to you part of the problem?

"Talking is part of the problem. Not because talk is bad, but because using logic to suppress your fear of uncertainty is hurtful to you, and that is what you often do when you talk. But listening to me or to your heart has never hurt you. Listening to fear—more specifically, shame—has robbed you of life. I want to invite you back to life again. You can always come talk to me about what you fear. It is not bad to be afraid. Let's acknowledge your fear and uncertainty and just keep living your life. Not running from the fear, and not agreeing with it. Not listening to it, and not drowning it out. Not forcing good thoughts, but inviting lovely ones and letting them do the duet with the thoughts that scare you so."

The Dictionary

When we're traumatized we avoid things.
Anything that reminds us of what hurt us stings.
But if we're truly to go test our wings
We must accept what hurt us, then find how it sings.
I'm not saying that we call trauma good
It's not good to suffer and it's not good to should.
But what I'm saying is we will find more healing
if we will touch our own pain and then find a new meaning.
One place I have started to look
for this healing is a special book
that most have on their shelf, but all have in their brain.
The dictionary can heal us, or make us insane!
There are so many words that scare me so,
and others with a new meaning that I now know.
Let me give an example—accountability.
I thought it meant shame; now it means, "Tell your story."
Here's another—it's judgment.
I thought it was punishment.
Shame was again, the definition.
So I couldn't trust my own vision,
believing that judgment couldn't be good.

If I was too sure of something, then I would should
on myself for being too judgmental.
But now I know judgment is unavoidable
and can be done in love, to set stories right,
to show people sweetness outside of their sight.
Faith is another word that once confused me.
I thought it was a rash indifference, a false certainty,
but now in this chapter I'm finally starting to see
that faith is uncertainty, communicated honestly
while choosing to follow your heart anyway
even when you don't know if you're going to be okay.
Another word is God—I thought, "Guy in the sky."
Now he's a Love in my heart who makes me want to fly.
So many more words are waiting to be freed
from bad definitions—joy, anger, lust, greed,
religion, rebellion, decision, imagination,
hope, frustration, imposition, invitation,
justice and cola, beauty and what's fair,
ownership, leadership, sin, and underwear.
The thingamajig is a virus overwriting my brain
changing every meaning to shame, shame, shame.
But the meaning of Love is still inside of my heart.
From this backup drive, I will reboot and restart
the sorry dictionary inside my head
to let words speak their beauty, to say new things instead.

Love is not a verb. Love is not a feeling. Love is not chemicals. Love is not kind actions. Love is not sex. Love is not advertising. Love is not doing the right thing. Love is not purity. Love is not sacrifice. Love is not selfishness. Love is not a whim. Love is not the sunshine. Love is not the air you breathe. Love is not music. Love is not your favorite number showing up on a clock. Love is not the universe. Love is not you.

Love is Love. And it's the smallest and biggest thing in the universe. Love cannot be arrived at by science or measured with the five senses. Love is not an experience.

Love is Love. It is invisible, inaudible, intangible. It is odorless, tasteless. It is infinite and inconceivable. And this is why some people (most people) don't truly believe in it. We have no patience for something that is invisible, inaudible, intangible. We want something we can experience, something we can know is true without a shadow of a doubt. We want something we can touch and smell. We want something we can reason to, something we can pick apart and dissect. We are suffering; we are dealing with problems too big for us to solve. We feel lost and hopeless and abandoned; we think we need a Love that is

physical and that will change what we're physically deal-
ing with each day. A Love that doesn't intervene in our
affairs or make things better is cheap, we say. And so we
continue to suffer believing that when things go our way,
we are "loved," and that when things don't go our way,
that we're "not," when in reality we feel deep down in-
side that we are not loved at all, even in our best moments,
for there is nothing that is both permanent and unchang-
ing as well as visible, audible, tangible, logical, physical,
or experiential to tell us that we're loved, and the thought
that Love might be invisible, inaudible, intangible, incom-
prehensible, metaphysical, and transcendental is repulsive
to a mind so wrapped up in the limited universe we can
see that it can see no other need for rescue beyond the
unsolvable physical and moral conundrums of our current
existence. For humanity's worst problem is not hunger,
or lack of resources, or war, or hate, or death, or climate
change, or greed, or corruption, or selfishness, or religion,
or godlessness. Humanity's worst problem is that we don't
believe in a Love that is big enough to carry us when we
are blind, deaf, and numb to its presence, a Love that still
kisses us when all of our mental faculties point to its ab-
sence, a Love that is still healing us even as our bodies
are being ripped to hamburger while the world watches
on and concludes we're gone forever, a Love that is so
radically inclusive that it even includes the realities that

seem to disprove its existence, a Love that is so real that it simply is, and summons our faith for no other reason than that it is Love—our heart's longing. Hence, the supreme irony of all the universe is that Love—the biggest thing of all—became the smallest, most invisible thing of all, that we might discover that Love is bigger than even sensation and experience themselves. And maybe in this discovery, a deeper healing beyond all the suffering of earthly life will take form—a healing for our own invisible, inaudible, intangible hearts.

That is the closest thing to a gospel that I believe.

Love is not a verb. Love is not a feeling. Love is not chemicals. Love is not music. But it includes ... all of those things.

Lust

I once thought it was sinful
For a human to feel sexual
Outside any sort of marital
bedtime routine
I once felt so awful
If I felt something sensual
But isn't it normal
to want love between?
Why have we got
to make lust a sin?
Involuntary thought,
knee-jerk feelings within?
What good is a law
Nobody can keep
when someone you saw
and you dream in your sleep?
We all have sinned,
Fallen short of the glory
of a God chagrined
that we obeyed our biology!
Absurdity can't be held for long,

so eventually I began to assume
I should at least *try* not to do wrong.
Feelings now and then didn't have to mean doom.
But the more I tried to direct thoughts away
the more they persisted; the more they would stay
"Please give me good thoughts" I would fearfully pray
And try to continue going about my day.
It wasn't too bad
Until I grew sad
Then I realized I had
a way to feel glad
with just imagination.
I was battling depression
and had no other solution
so I started masturbation
and never could stop
Now I felt evil,
just like the glop
coming out of my shameful
thing down below.
How to control it, I didn't know.
The more I avoided it, the more it came.
I held it in enough to cause physical pain.
My entire identity was nothing but shame.
Jesus said just one look was the same as adultery.
I thought it was true, so I thought I was ugly

like a rapist violating dozens of people.
You can find pretty faces even under the steeple.
I put my phone on the other side of the house
But the power was too strong, so I crept like a mouse
And did my thing, and put it right back.
Even without tech, impure thoughts I don't lack.
Should I be castrated?
Shame never abated.
I felt so deflated,
dirty, contaminated.
Many mornings at breakfast, I'd sit in my chair
teetering on the edge, because I wouldn't dare
Risk the chance that somebody else would sit there
And smell what I'd done the night before in the air.
I felt so much guilt
For the pictures I saw
while under my quilt;
so I began to draw
thinking it was less wrong than pictures that were real.
But I was scared of my artwork a very great deal.
I'd delete or destroy, then later remake.
I wouldn't dare throw my girl in the trash, so I'd take
her into the sink and make mush out of paper.
I couldn't risk letting someone else find her later.
And before you assume the words of my rhyme
are talking about porn, you're wrong; this whole time

I had never seen nakedness, only clothes worn.
I hadn't even started looking at true porn!
The first time I did, it was something I drew—
what some parts should look like I had little clue.
It was quickly deleted, then drawn again new.
I loved it so much and hated it too.
One day I was talking with H.L.
while picking at acne in front of the sink.
My knees nearly buckled and I nearly fell
when he said to me with a smile and a wink
"I want you to put your face on display,
"with all that crud and everything."
Soon I realized what he really did say,
and I felt fear's familiar unending sting.
I knew exactly which crud he was talking about
And I answered in my brain with a frightened shout,
"Oh no!
"Absolutely not!
"I couldn't show
"Such awful rot!
"There is no way
"I could put *her* on display!"
Later we talked about the stories I write
and I spoke of my favorite one, beautiful and bright.
Then H.L. suggested
the book should be illustrated.

"I'm not the angry God you think
"I don't wash your crud down the sink
"I love how you smell! To me, you don't stink.
"I like dresses, too, whether they're red or pink.
"As it turns out, this whole time you were learning
"To honor your dreams! Your hunger and yearning
"Is the very same feeling that brought you to me!
"I want you to come out of the dark and paint freely.
"You insist you can't draw but you know that's not true—
"Every moment you suffered, every picture you drew
"Was part of my art class; you did faithfully study
"every curve, every line of the human body.
"You were never a rapist—
"how absurd! You're an artist!"
It took many years more
shame's voice to ignore
The healing isn't done,
but by now, I can have fun
with the thoughts in my head
and the feelings in my bed
and let them be
whatever to me
is sweet and pretty
for me to see.
My own sexuality
is no longer my enemy.

I could not run away.
I am glad; it will stay.

Gravity

What would you do
if gravity stopped holding you?
You say it never would,
but it actually could.
You believe it will,
because it holds you still
and has always done so.
But you don't really know
if tomorrow it will be.
All we have is probability,
our thought and feeling,
and faith in this or the other thing.
Some things are likely,
some things are absurdity,
but all things are mystery.
When this you see truly,
you'll have the humility
to accept possibility
of being the wrong one.
It can even be fun
to be clueless and learning.

Honor your own yearning
for mystery and adventure
by being unsure.
You don't know anything—
now you can sing!
You can make any human your friend
if you don't have a hill to defend.
You can put faith in love
without a word from above
because it's beautiful to you!
What else would you do
in a world where everyone acts
like they have the facts
while no one knows what's true?
It's not up to you
what is fiction or real.
Certainly don't conceal
the facts, science, and study
that makes the waters less muddy.
But know there are limits to your sight.
You see just a few stars of the trillions in the night,
held in place not by rules, but by reality.
Whatever that is, we've still yet to see.

What if the entire story of evolution and death and survival of the fittest was a story about a planet—that is estranged and believes it is not loved—journeying to discover love? Humans are not more valuable than animals, but are the first creatures to glimpse their hearts again, leading to music, poetry, art, science, leading to greater highs and lower lows than any other species. For unlike the animals, the anesthesia has finally worn off, and we know we are broken. That is the first step of healing, and arguably the most difficult, and of course, painful.

Isn't it strange that love calls us away from the survival of the fittest mindset? The mindset that ensured the existence of our species?

Does this hypothesis mean that as the world as a whole discovers love, we will discover other worlds? The universe is barren. Is there a winderverse out there?

"The models and constructs and principles we impose upon the universe do little to promote understanding. They help us operate in the universe in a way that is partially effective, which is why we persist in defending our ideas even when people are getting hurt. Love doesn't ask us to have our facts in a row; it asks us to embrace the truth. Order helps us function. Mystery helps us understand."

– From the unfinished story *The Winderanium*

Strangeness

Have you ever just stopped
and felt the Strangeness of it all?
Here we are, plopped
in the middle of nowhere, on a spinning ball,
falling around a fire, in a Beautiful world,
living our lives not remembering being born
and everywhere we go, always encircled
by more Strangeness—an ever-present thorn
to remind us that we might be wrong entirely
about not just our world, but all of infinity.
Don't think about it too much or you might need therapy.
Just breathe in the Strangeness and enjoy its eccentricity.
Explanations hold allure,
but reality is bolder
than the few facts we rearrange
when so little we know.
One thing's for sure—
As I grow older,
The world doesn't get less strange;
It only seems more so.

Is the Winderverse true?

"It is; and so are you!"

I don't know what to do.

"Live like it's true."

But what if it's not?

"That's preposterous to my thought."

But why shouldn't it false be?

"There's so much you don't see."

How do I embrace uncertainty?

"You don't. You plant a tree."

In the ocean it will drown!

"It will never fall down."

Does that make me ungood? To be so?

"Nothing could."

I am Loved and it's true, though how, I haven't a clue.

"Someday you will grasp the sweet mystery of the shoe."

Evolution

In my quest for information
I realized the facts of evolution
and now I am lost with no solution
wondering why death and natural selection
should be the reason every living thing
can eat and sleep and dance and sing.
If we were created by survival of the fittest
why shouldn't we kill off all but the worthiest
of our species and yours, and all of the rest?
If death is our maker then why is it best
to love or be kind unless it suits us?
In despair I found myself saying thus,
when in truth I know nothing, or at least very little.
My fears are great and my faith is brittle.
I want to trust science and say what is true
but what if science says there's no point to me and you?
Do I choose truth or love? What do I do?
Are there any third options to consider too?
If your very own parent says you were a mistake,
does that make you feel loved or groaning sounds make?
If your very own universe says you're a fluke,

is believing in love any better than puke?
If love is just chemicals acting in my brain,
then love can be anesthetized just as with pain.
But it already is, 'cause why do you think
all over the world humans act like they stink?
Maybe love is a deeper thing beyond spacetime
a thing we express in chemicals, hugs, and rhyme,
but a thing that is nevertheless quite its own being—
a thing that goes beyond the world's way of seeing.
Every time a little critter underwent changes
or gained new organs or new phalanges
perhaps it thought itself strange or weird—
and yet each aberration leads not to what's feared,
but instead leads to progress to be enjoyed and shared
with new generations of creatures who are far less scared
to accept the changes of the last pioneer
until they too must face changes and steer
the future to new places and ways of existence.
And perhaps through millions of years of resistance
to old ways of being, new ways take shape.
Just as we ditched egg-laying we've also ditched rape.
We once swam in oceans and now we visit space.
We used to have tribes and now we respect race.
Every good thing came from ditching the old,
the entire story of life did unfold
as a story of rebellion against status quo

so that new ways of living and being we could know.
And now here I am, wondering if Love is real,
thinking about Something Strange that I feel.
Am I an aberration? I'm greatly afraid
that this stuff about Love is a puke that I made.

Excerpt from the unfinished story *The Winderanium*

At length, they spoke. "The ocean is beautiful, isn't it? And strange."

I nodded. "Definitely. Definitely both."

"Some people say that the ocean has been explored even less than outer space."

"Do you think that's true?" I questioned.

They turned towards me and smiled. "How do you know what is left to be explored if you haven't explored it yet?" My companion leaned over and picked up a seashell. "Come walk with me. We must collect the shells."

I followed behind my new friend, though honestly they felt more like an old friend by now. They felt like someone I had known most of my life, and yet had just met. They felt so familiarly unfamiliar that I felt compelled to follow along and pick up shells, though I had no idea why we should do such an unnecessary task at all when by all appearances we barely knew each other.

"I was curious if you might know where we are?" I asked them at length.

"I do," they replied. "Don't you?"

"I'm afraid I don't," I told them, leaning down to pick

up a shell.

The person nodded. "You're on the edge of the ocean."

"Which one? Which beach?"

"There's only one ocean. They're all connected, you know."

I stepped backward quickly as the icy water unexpectedly darted up and kissed my toes before rushing back again to where it had started.

"The water likes you," my companion remarked. "But it is also shy, and fiercely passionate at the same time."

I observed the surf continuing to vacillate, first moving forward bravely to display its passion, but then a few moments later hurrying backward in fright.

"That sounds like something I experience a lot," I admitted. "I'm always trying to figure out what to do to be loved."

My friend nodded knowingly. "There is always the fear, in the presence of someone you love, that your passion will be seen—and there is always the fear that it won't. But love can happen even where two fears dance." Then with glee, they spotted another shell and picked it up triumphantly.

I soaked in these words for a moment as another wave soaked my feet. The tide was rising at a snail's pace, growing in courage moment by moment as it began to express more fully its love.

"The water goes back and forth a lot. But it certainly doesn't seem wishy-washy like me."

"It's okay to be wishy-washy," my friend answered with scarcely a thought. "Not that I think you actually are. And keep in mind, the ocean is a liquid, and you're not."

I laughed. I loved watching the ocean. I loved watching it dance. It was strong, magical, lovely. And in this moment, I realized there might be something strangely beautiful about my back-and-forthness. For without the dance of the tide, the ocean would be just a lake dreaming.

"I—I'm sick of being afraid all the time. I have to tell you, I am afraid almost every moment of my life. I am afraid to do anything at all, and afraid to do the opposite. I am afraid to get up in the morning and go to bed at night, afraid to say hello and afraid to say bye, afraid to be seen and afraid not to, afraid to be alone and afraid to be together, afraid of looking one way and afraid of looking the other. And I don't know why."

"The why is often hidden in our story, a story that needs time to heal," said my companion, stopping to pick up another shell. "There is very little you can do about your feelings or your fear, besides eating ice cream of course, or crying, or yelling, or going on a walk. But there's a lot you can do about your dreams."

The wind howling across the waves grew louder. I almost expected it to speak.

"I don't know if I have any dreams."

"You do."

My lip quivered. "I have dreams. But I'm afraid of them, too."

"It's okay to be afraid." My friend dipped their toe in the water, but the water rushed away. "The ocean is afraid, too. But it continues to waltz—two steps forward, one step back, until the high tide has been fulfilled. The ways you express your dreams—your stories, your art, your friend-ships, your comings and goings and doings—are no dif-ferent."

Knowing for Sure

I need to know, and know for sure
And hence is my great plight—
I need to know, and know for sure
If my beliefs are right
So I can know, and know for sure
If my thinking is watertight
So I can know, and know for sure
If my behavior is alright
So I can know, and know for sure
If I am lovely in others' sight
So I can maybe know for sure
If I am good and bright.
But though the need holds much allure
It is not a need; it is a desired height
Of knowledge to give me an impossible cure
For the worries that give me such a fright.
These worries forever I will endure
Unless I trust a love hidden by night,
The magic and uncertainty of following winder,
And a Something Strange that can't be known in the light.
I will never know if my beliefs are true or false,

So I might as well listen to my heart's own pulse.
But do I even have a heart?
I might be just a fart
In a moment of time
Expressing its smell through rhyme.
Whatever its cause
I will trust my own smell
Because nothing can pause
Dominoes that already fell
And continue to tumble.
I wish to be humble
I wish to be loved
But I'm pushed and I'm shoved
By the forces of nature.
How can I be mature
If I'm still just a sapling
Truly knowing nothing?
Why do I worry about any of this at all?
Because I need to know, and know for sure
That I'm good and bright; is it worth it to fall
In love with a mist
Such as myself
That cannot be kissed?
So I search the bookshelf
In pursuit of answers and meaning and belonging
To satisfy my fears and my own heart's longing.

And yet everywhere I sail
Is utterly to no avail.
I am confused.
I am abused.
I am enthused
By illusions of being anything else.
I have no hope
So how do I cope?
I will face my fear
And lose the lies I hold dear
And try my best to be sincere.
If love is real, it will hear.
But now do I seek love to earn
By my own sincerity?
The love for which I yearn
Will for its own sake accept me.

I don't know the truth. Instead I need to go live my truth. That may make me a bad person, but in so doing I will discover if I'm really Loved. I long for the kind of love that sticks around not just when I'm good and deserving of it but when I'm bad. The only way to know I have that love is for the love to be tested.

Estrangement

Dear Dad,
I'm mad
And sad,
And I feel bad
About being gone.
What if I'm wrong?
What have I done?
I'm the wayward son
From the prodigal tale
But you stand on the porch
Not to hug me, but to rail
At my sins and scorch
Me with a question.
You beg me for an answer.
I know your intention
Is to ignore your own cancer
That was eating me alive
From the inside out
And made me writhe—
But I couldn't shout
Because you wouldn't let me

Be myself.
I tip-toed timidly
Across a shelf
Of knives, but you
Said you were waiting
For me to drop the shoe!
Your ego deflating
Was too much to bear.
You didn't want the truth.
No guilt could you share.
I confronted you about a tooth,
But I wish I had kept silent.
I wanted to hear you say sorry;
Instead I unleashed a storm violent
By mumbling for four minutes nervously
So you could complain for four hours
About how my whole family
Was knocking down your towers.
Is this how you see me?
Are we the Axis powers
Undermining your authority?
You say I left you without a word.
I did—but wouldn't you find it absurd
To ask a little injured bird
To make its reasons for departure heard
Before it could fly away from a deaf man?

You say you want my reason
For running away from the frying pan?
You say I'm guilty of treason;
I say I'm too sick to stay.
It wasn't one big thing; it was many things
You thought I had demons to pray away
But all you did was cut off my wings.
You're addicted to having things figured out.
And for this reason, so am I.
You're addicted to being in control of all doubt
So you'll never fall, and never fly.
You told me, "You're going to do it.
"You're not going to try.
"You'll do it just this way—
"Reach for the sky."
But nobody succeeds without failure
Nobody grows under censure.
I tried to be nice and pretty
When I spoke of your failings
But you saw through my insincerity
And greeted me with wailings
Of wanting to know my fact
While you continued to act
Like you were faultless, to cover your shame.
What good is my truth when you play a game?
But now, perhaps, my deepest regret

Is that I didn't let you have it.
I didn't give myself the benefit
Of speaking up, but I was unfit
To do so; I was too scared
So I wouldn't have dared.
You would never have healed if I had yelled;
Only your ego would have been felled
And quickly restored to its former glory
By your distorted version of the story
That keeps you from seeing your very own soul
So your ego can always remain in control.
Yet I still wish I had spoken and argued bravely
For my own sake, so my own words could maybe have
healed me.
So here are my words, spoken in love for myself to see—
I am so, so, fucking angry!
And before you say
That it's not okay
For me to express
myself this way,
Let me impress
Upon you my needs.
Stop trying to help me!
Stop planting your seeds
Of wisdom-turned-folly.
Stop pulling my weeds!

You don't know a lily
From a cockroach, so please
Stay warm when it's chilly;
Stay warm and don't freeze.
I need you to heal,
But the man who I love
Is a corpse who can't feel
And won't budge if I shove.
I once had a nightmare
Of trying to wake you,
But you acted like I wasn't there
And now I haven't a clue
How to reach you, because
Every time I try to speak
My brain turns to fuzz
And my body feels weak.
Daddy, wake up!
I'm going to throw up!
I'm finding my way up
Out of the mud you churned up!
I know your brain is angry
But is your heart proud of me?
If you knew how much I struggled inside
To become who I am, in spite of your lies,
Would you open your eyes, would your heart brim with
pride?

Oh, daddy, please, please don't close your eyes!
If I caught all the stars
Would you know the difference?
If we ended the wars
In our heads, could we fix this?
You live behind bars,
Yet forget your sad entrance.
You are confused.
You feel abused.
And so do I.
I know both of us cry.
So who is right
And who is wrong?
We both have a plight.
Our suffering is long,
But you think it's only you.
And I think that is why the shoe
Is being dropped by the one who is too
Obsessed with being right to care
If his sons and his daughter are even aware
That he's human, not god, and yet everywhere
Surrounded by sunshine and birds that sing.
You don't have to change a single thing.
Just stop trying to change me!
Many years have gone by without your meddling
And I'm not the way I used to be.

You would find me today to be terribly unsettling
For I walk new roads and search for greener grass
Than what I had in your world that you're too scared to
leave.
If you met me today, perhaps you would pass
On who I am without putting me through your sieve.
Though you already did in your world before.
You filtered out the bad; you've always kept score
Of the ways we could fail you, the calamities in store,
For such was your trauma in days of yore.
You were constantly inferior
In the eyes of your superior.
You ache in your interior
Because your dad was a stickler
For the kind of man who is always right—
And that is what you have become in your own sight
To spare yourself of the pain
Of upsetting your dad's idol again.
I will honor you
By following what's true,
By being brave enough to lose
My entire identity, and I choose
To be myself by losing myself,
To leave you playing games by yourself,
To hope one day you will heal yourself
By finding the sunshine that lies in the deep,

In the places of the heart we visit in our sleep.
Maybe one day you'll give my mom back her Jeep.
Maybe one day you'll stop and look at the heap
Of lies about love and identity you believe.
You'll face the terror of throwing away your sieve
And smelling all things as they are; first you'll see
A pile of rubble, filth, shame, and pain.
Don't stay there; go deeper, and then you'll be free.
For in the depths of your heart is a sun casting rain
On thirsty deserts full of hurting people
Injured by the god of the pulpit and steeple.
You once said God was not my father
You once said God was not my old man.
You said he wasn't someone I had to be afraid to bother.
You said he wasn't just a chum or a fan.
You said he was someone I could call dad.
Now I don't even know if he's real, good, or bad.
But what I do know is that I am so, so sad
Because you might have been all I truly had.

"I have a new principle to teach you about. It's called 'the uncertainty principle.' It says whoever is the least certain is the closest to telling the truth."

But I'm totally certain that $2 + 2 = 4$, and that's totally true. Your principle is arbitrary.

"I have another principle to teach you about. It's called 'the arbitrary principle.' It says that the truth about anyone's story will always sound arbitrary if you didn't know it before."

Uh… You can't be serious. But it's actually starting to make sense.

Wisdom

I've been obsessed with being wise,
which has actually led me into more lies
about who I really am and what I'm here for.
I can't listen to the voice of wisdom any more!
If wisdom is more shouldn'ts and another should
Give me folly instead; it would be more good!
I'm drowning in rules
this world pushes and pulls
and makes me feel dumb
so then I feel glum
so then I feel even worse
for not dissecting my own curse
and figuring out how
to feel better now!
I've been obsessed with doing right
which has caused me such a terrible fright
because everything I do could potentially hurt someone
somehow—
I'm exhaling carbon dioxide and causing climate change
right now!
What my therapist has helped me see

is that this overcriticism is OCD
and that it doesn't reflect the truth of me—
but the only truth I have is subjectivity
and it's technically true
that I exhale CO_2,
so I want to protest.
But instead, it would be best
for me to be kind
to my body and mind.
I would never criticize the deeds
of any other person with needs
showing themselves care.
But for myself, if I dare,
I feel evil and unworthy,
but I must care for myself extravagantly
or I will never heal.
Regardless of what I feel
I must honor my dreams a great deal
and care for my needs and desires.
Meanwhile, I see all the fires
and blame my actions or lack thereof.
Yet in the face of blame, I must also meet love
and realize the lies.
I matter in your eyes,
and that is enough.
I don't need to earn love

or be a great hero
to become more than zero—
because I already am,
but I don't know why.
Love feels like a scam
if I didn't at least try
to earn it somehow.
But I deserve love right now,
not because I'm invincible,
or invisible
or totally ethical
or kind, or practical,
but because I just do!
But why should it be true?
Well let me tell you a secret.
If you keep rewinding for a bit,
you'll see every effect has a cause.
And we feel unloved because
we think love is an effect.
If I did this or that perfect,
if I was successful or pretty,
now people will want me!
But for no other reason than my own sanity
I believe Love is a cause that created me—
not the universe, time, or my body
but my heart you cannot see,

and for this reason alone, I am worthy.
I have hyper-responsibility
but there's no way to calculate
what my responsibility *should* be
so instead I analyze and berate.
I don't have to do right
to be worthy in Love's sight.
But then I analyze whether Love is real at all
and once more into rumination I fall
trying to calculate whether there's anything true
besides us and this universe and the things that we do.
Maybe I could be content with the affection
of other humans—love without perfection
which is beautiful and sweet, when I see it clearly,
which is never at all, because the thingamajig convinces
me
that their love would dissipate if I did something bad,
and I do bad all the time, so then I get mad
and assume love doesn't even exist.
For the sake of my life, I must persist
in assuming people love me somewhere in the Deep
even when people get mad at me, leave me, or bleep,
Or else I'll be always tied to what I see
on the surface, the anger of people frustrated with me.
Although most people really aren't frustrated at all—
once more it's the thingamajig making me feel small

plastering shame and lies
over what I see with my eyes
to convince me its own way of seeing
is more valid than my heart's way of being.
All is subjective in this universe.
Nothing is wrong, nothing perverse
except that which doesn't correspond with your heart—
the love that we express, but only in part
because we're finite animals on a hurtling sphere
trying to communicate with those we hold dear
something too beautiful and infinite for this planet.
So I try to say, "I love you," and instead I say, "Dammit!"
You're going to have to give me the benefit
of the doubt on this one; words are unfit
to demonstrate the love we all know but can't see
as we run around trying to prove perfectly
that we are perfect in a world that ensures that we're not.
That we're lovely in the Deep when we look like we're rot.
And so what can we do? Let's just give ourselves a lot
of grace to be here where we are with what we've got.
We have little to nothing, except a longing
for a winderverse of infinite belonging.
If somebody is poor and steals some bread,
could we truly say they did something bad?
If somebody needs to breathe the air to live,
would we condemn them for any CO_2 they would give?

If I need to eat lots of food to survive,
if I need to pick flowers and create artwork to thrive,
if I need to eat a cow, and not donate to charity
to feel full and feel loved, and have enough for me
to attempt to pursue the dreams deep inside,
would it be good to exhort me myself to deride?
I need to know that I'm Loved when I'm "bad."
I need to know my needs will not make others mad
if I show them in full force,
which is why, of course,
I must stay in this world so I can discover
that in the face of inadequacy there is a Lover
or many, who will care about me even right here
in the scariest of places, in the center of my fear.
Wisdom is not about knowing what's true.
Wisdom is not about knowing what to do.
Wisdom is not about living your life unafraid.
Wisdom is not figuring out which band-aid
will make yourself "good" when you already are.
Wisdom is not knowing the chemistry of a star.
Wisdom is not knowing; it's not knowledge at all.
Wisdom is not ignoring; it's not putting up a wall.
Wisdom is being in the center of mystery
without knowledge or ignorance, just sensitivity
to Love behind the things that you know and you don't.
Wisdom is not knowing whether you should or you won't.

Wisdom is not rules;
it's the jewels
in your heart.
Wisdom is not what you say or impart.
Wisdom is the way you play in the rain
when the thingamajig says you messed up again.
Wisdom is the way you laugh at the table,
even when you don't know if Love's more than a fable.
Wisdom isn't pretending;
it's just the attempting
to live like there's Love
and live like you're enough.

The Right Thing

From the unfinished story The Duet

When I try to do the right thing,
I find I cannot even sing.
When I try to say myself I'll be,
I find all along I was always me.

"There is no right or ethical thing to do. My only concern is that everyone knows they are fully loved as they are, where they are."

Do you succeed?

"Not yet. You can't make someone feel loved. You can only leave them flowers."

But if you do that the flowers will die.

"They will. It's worth it for love."

My Nightmare

Everything I do is a loathsome thorn,
Injuring someone somehow.
Oh how I wish I had never been born!
But what can I do about that now?
If I killed myself that would be a thorn too,
Hurting those I care about and love.
But that care won't repair the things that I do
In this world of pain, push, and shove.
It is impossible to do what is loving or right,
And nothing is fully love or fully good.
We all do what is best in our own sight,
While love itself doesn't shine like it should.
Shouldn't the world be a blank canvas empty,
waiting for us to paint love's worth?
Instead it's a river flowing steady,
Ready to sweep paint off the earth!
The earth gave you your days,
And hath taken them away.
Let the name of blind physics receive praise!
What then shall I say?
How then shall I act

If love cannot be expressed in fact?
I know I've found love inside my dreams
But is love also in my nightmares?
This world is a nightmare, or so it seems;
A place engineered so uncaring it scares
Me into believing there is no love at all.
Or at least if there is, it's so very small.
If I can't find love in the dark,
What good is love in the light?
The difference between the worlds is stark—
One is too dark to see in and the other too bright.
Can you tell which I crave?
I can give you a clue.
Love in Strange I could brave;
Beauty without love is poo.
But we've almost got this world figured out, do we not?
We've discovered physics and evolution
And realized we all are flotsam born from rot.
All hail the great scientific revolution!
Now we know there's no meddling Being
Out there winning us into a new kind of seeing.
We've got info; who needs meaning?
And all the while we're too numb for perceiving
That maybe we're right about everything but not true.
Maybe we're both accident and treasure
At the same time—it is good you are you!

Maybe there's no way in this world love to measure,
And yet love holds us close at the same time
In the darkest of dark and the brightest of bright,
In the places we're blind, whispering to us in rhyme
So that even when there isn't a speck of love in sight
Even in a world where everything is sin,
We will find faith in nightmares that love will still win.

Philosophy

Before I can rest, before I can sleep
I always must sort through a terrible heap
Of meaningless questions, or so I now see,
for they do not make sense, except only to me!
How short is a moment
And how long is forever?
Do limits have limits?
Can something be never?
What is isn't, and what was was?
What is was now? I need to know, because
if I don't know whether my thoughts are yellow or pink
I will no longer even be able to think!
The questions are good, the asking is okay,
but sometimes there are no true answers to say!

Ethics

Ethics are impossible to calculate
And disastrous to ignore.
I don't know who to imitate,
But I guess disaster's in store.
I sure tried at any rate.
Please love me! Don't be sore!

"I am ready," he said, "to draw you out of the houses where you hide, and make you a home. A home that will follow you throughout the world into every house you enter."

– H.L. in the unfinished story *The Heart's Longing*

My Dilemma

I keep looking for a sign
that everything's going to turn out fine.
I keep hoping for a way to know
that Love is present in spite of every sorrow.
But what I'm searching for
is an assurance above my floor.
I could never hope to reach
the level of knowledge I hope to teach.
So maddening it is, so simple a question,
yet the answer is absent, or beyond my digestion.
And so I'm faced with these two choices—
listen to the fray, to the darkness and its voices,
or accept this blind faith in a ridiculous dream
and trust that this world is not what it may seem.

Here's a Cookie

"My darling love,

"you thought your choices

"were only two—

"below or above,

"blind faith or dark voices,

"the red pill or blue.

"I'm hear to say

"that you'll find your way.

"You wonder what to do.

"You wonder what is true.

"Taste the winder; I love you.

"Nobody's going to drop the shoe.

"You ask me questions, but dear little kid,

"there's more than puzzlement; come open the lid.

"Come see the stars; here's a cookie to eat.

"Your worries matter but your smile is sweet.

"Neither high nor low will do.

"Neither knowledge nor ignorance will save you.

"My pill is a rainbow

"and no matter what you don't know

"love will surely show

"wherever you go.

"It's okay to be here

"in the hallway you fear.

"Even in a hall with only two doors

"you can always dance across the floors

"into a deeper space inside your heart

"a place you can laugh and scream and fart

"because love accepts you as you are.

"You don't have to know the chemistry of a star

"to feel its warmth in the black of night.

"My darling dear, you're going to be alright.

"Your eyes are tired and bleary and red.

"Let me kiss you and send you off to bed."

One night, while I was anxious about my racing thoughts, H.L. interrupted me with an answer that was off-topic in the most lovely way. He showed me the beautiful stars outside the window scattered across a clear sky. Then he reminded me of the story of Abraham, how he was asked to count the stars and the sand.

"Look at the stars. Try to count them, if you can. As many as the stars in the sky, so will your blessings be, like the rain falling down on you. Every drop of water is a major blessing in your life. There will be so many drops that for every five that run off your coat, ten more will dance in your hair. You will not hold your gifts tightly the way you would if there were only a few. You'll have so many that you won't be able to hold them all even if you wanted to. You'll learn to live an open-handed, free life! This is my promise to you!"

I was taken aback by his statement and didn't know what to make of it. Several months later, he started showing me what the stars really were. Each one was a perspective shift, a conversation, a friend, and over the course of the next year they multiplied and I started to lose count. It was through this process that H.L. helped me through one of the hardest chapters of my life.

* * *

"For every star, there will be a corresponding butterfly."

H.L. said this to me as we counted the stars. It's been several years since we did that regularly.

A few months ago, I found myself in the ER during one of the worst chapters of my life.

"Now it's time to start counting the butterflies," he whispered shortly thereafter.

And I'm starting to notice the smallest ways in which my perspectives on my life, my pain, and my world are starting to shift. Little glimpses, little gifts, little reminders that things aren't always what they seem. Or that sometimes, something that looks one way can transform into something quite the opposite...

That process isn't finished yet. It's still happening. It's an unfinished story.

But as I've found myself caring for my own needs better,

allowing myself to feel what I feel, and challenging my own perspective on my pain, I have found myself more free to express myself and take risks.

This book exists because of the stars, the rain, and the butterflies.

You are Loved

        Deeply

           Fully

              Exquisitely

      Incomprehensibly

  Deservedly

         Winderfully

              Terribly

                Much

Opening for the unfinished story *The Heart's Longing*

People have said, many times, the same—
they can hear the wind calling their name.
He whispers lovingly through the air
to every porch-dweller in their chair.
Imagination is captured
and hearts are raptured.
They've fallen in love, and want him again.
They know they will see him but never know when.
Sometimes in the sun, in a laugh, in a song—
he draws them in close and they dance along.
A meaning arrives none dare understand.
But it fills each drop of water and each grain of sand.
Aliveness is here, and a sense of belonging.
For the voice has called us into our Heart's Longing.

Six-year-old Hazel was much the same. She was coloring on her porch, when the wind called her name.

He drew her away from her crayons and her book. He drew her away from the shadowy nook. He drew her away from the yard—past the fence. The wonder of the world had just grown too intense.

After crossing the street was the park right next door. She knew where she was—she had been here before. She would play on the playground, like little kids do. And the world all around her would become something new.

Her shirt would extend into a beautiful gown. The stick in her hand would become a sword or a crown. The slides became mountains, the jungle gym trees, the seesaw a boat as she sailed through the breeze.

And today, much the same as always she did, she believed in these things, and had fun being a kid. Then with beautiful grace and tender care came a quieting presence and the voice of the air . . .

* * *

"Hazel," came the gentle exhalation of the wind.

Hazel perked up, wonder filling her eyes. She knew the voice that was calling her—a voice she had always known, a voice that spoke to her in the stillness of her dreams.

"I'm right here!" she said excitedly.

The wind grew louder, rustling through the grass and rushing through the trees, circling around her and drawing her close. The sun grew bright as the sparkle in her eyes—overwhelming enough to bring all things to an end, but beautiful enough to bring all things to their beginning. And from this light stepped forward a certain somebody.

Hazel recognized his eyes immediately—they looked just like her own eyes. But the joy in his smile was quite unlike anything she could remember seeing before.

"I am delighted to meet you!" Hazel exclaimed. "I've always wanted to meet you, you know."

"You have always known me, dear. And I am delighted to be with you!"

Hazel jumped forward and gave him a hug.

"What is your name?" she asked him after a long moment's silence.

"I am your Heart's Longing," answered the Heart's Longing. "I am just—well, you know—just me."

"Can I call you H.L. for short?" Hazel's gaze pierced straight through the fire in his eyes.

H.L. laughed. "You certainly may."

They spent several minutes strolling through the park together, picking up cool leaves and watching the squirrels. Hazel discovered a very handsome pinecone, but was somewhat alarmed by its stickiness. H.L., on the other hand, discovered a very helpful drinking fountain where she was able to wash up. Then they took turns cupping their hands at the fountain while the other would prepare to run away from the impending splash the moment the fountain turned off. When they grew tired of this, they collapsed in a fit of giggles on the side of the hill.

"You're goofy!" Hazel scolded.

"It was your idea," H.L. argued.

"No, it was yours! And now I'm all wet!" She was trying to feign seriousness, but finally burst into more laughter.

"Hazel, I have a very special surprise for you," H.L. announced.

Hazel stood up. "Ice cream?"

"We'll do ice cream tomorrow." H.L. stood up, too. "Today is something else—something more special."

"More special than ice cream?" Hazel pretended to be confused.

H.L. smiled. "More special than the stars, my dear." At that moment, H.L. produced a little white book with embroidered flowers, which he gave to Hazel. She flipped it open with gusto, pleased to find that the book was written in H.L.'s own handwriting (which she recognized right away) and that there were sticker sheets included. The gift was indeed very special.

"Is it a storybook?" Hazel inquired.

"Yes, it is. It's our story."

Hazel flipped to the end of the book, where she encountered a great many empty pages. "Are you going to finish it?"

"We are going to finish it together," clarified H.L. "And decorate it, too."

After affixing a smiley face sticker to page one, she

gave the book to H.L., who placed a heart-shaped sticker on the cover. They both declared the book perfect.

"Let's go inside the house and get some apple juice!" H.L. suggested. Hazel agreed that it was a delicious proposal. So they hop-skipped across the street, past the fence, through the yard, onto the porch, and into the house.

"Honey, don't track dirt on the carpet!" Hazel's mom scolded.

"Oh," Hazel said glumly. "Sorry Mommy." She cast a glance towards H.L., who was failing miserably at hiding a laugh behind his sudden frown. This made Hazel feel much better. She slid off her shoes, watching while H.L. proceeded through the living room without bothering at all to take off his own.

"You're setting a bad example!" Hazel scolded him.

Hazel's mother chuckled. "I know, sweetie. I really shouldn't care so much about the carpet. Don't worry about it—you're not in trouble."

Hazel and H.L. exchanged glances.

"I need to get this cake done in time for your daddy's birthday tomorrow," she continued. "Then we've got to go to the store and run some errands and stuff."

Hazel quadruple-bounced through the living room and into the kitchen, where she and H.L. skated in their socks across the sleek, linoleum floor until they crashed into the refrigerator. Hazel whipped out the apple juice and proceeded to pour a glass for herself and a glass for H.L. Meanwhile, Hazel's mother started whipping up frosting for the cake she was making, paying the other two little attention.

"You must have been really excited to give me my book!" Hazel seated herself at the kitchen island.

H.L. sat down as well. "Yes, I was very excited. I've been writing it since before you were born."

"What will the next chapter be about?"

A tinge of sorrow marked H.L.'s voice. "We are going to finish up this chapter first."

"And then what?"

H.L. hesitated. "The next chapter will be a sad chapter."

"Super sad?"

"Yes—very much so."

Hazel stared down at her socks. "How come?"

"Every story has sad chapters, my dear. But this next chapter is not the last chapter, and that's what matters." Observing a frosting bowl nearby, H.L. dipped his finger in and took a lick.

"Hazel!" scolded her mom. "Don't stick your fingers in my frosting!"

"I didn't do it!" Hazel insisted.

Her mother went back to her work.

"You're getting me in trouble H.L.!" Hazel whispered. "Though I think I'd rather be in trouble for something you did than for something I did."

"I'd rather be in trouble together," H.L. chimed in.

"What are you whispering about over there?" Hazel's mother questioned, turning towards them. She picked up H.L.'s cup. "Sweetie, who's this for?"

"That's H.L.'s apple juice Mommy!"

Hazel's mom showed some interest. "Whose?"

"H.L.'s," Hazel explained, putting her arm around him (as he did the same). "He's my best friend."

All traces of both confusion and interest immediately disappeared. "Oh," her mother said carefully. "Well—maybe, uh, maybe you and Ayjel can go do chores together." She immediately went back to her work.

Hazel had already wondered if her mother could see H.L. She could scarcely imagine any grown-up being able to see him, considering how they always seemed so preoccupied with "stuff." Then again, maybe there were a few grown-ups who were different.

Hazel scooted out of the kitchen, with H.L. following closely behind. She peeked over her shoulder just in time to see her mother pour H.L.'s apple juice back into the jug.

"Great," Hazel complained. "Now everybody is going to get your germs." She paused. "Actually, do you even have germs?"

"Oh yes," H.L. answered. "But mine are the good kind."

The Whisper

Why are you so quiet
when my head is so noisy?
I need you to speak up a bit
so dark thoughts won't control me!

Instead you just whisper
like the wind in the trees.
I can't find the winder
until I listen to the breeze.

I'm begging you to shout!
Strike me with a blast of lightning!
Interrupt the megaphone of doubt!
Yet you say it would be too frightening.

If you spoke too much in the bombs and the clamor,
I would never run away to the quiet wood.
You invite me to a gentle stream to lay down my armor.
I drink of your softness and find I am good.

I want you to speak to me in my worst hour

so I will not suffer and will not be afraid.
You want the same, so you leave me a flower
and tell me some words from a poem you made.

But I don't hear a word 'til I go to the stream.
In darkest of places shouldn't faintest stars gleam?
And they do! You're not mute; I am blind as a bat.
I cry out on my bed but all I see is my stuffed cat.

Can't you do something?
Can't you make me hear?
I'm afraid to take wing—
there's nothing wrong with my ear!

Sometimes I think I want to fly,
but if I really did I would scream.
I want to but I'm not ready to try.
I'm too scared, so I'll sit here and dream.

And such is the tragic human condition.
We want love to lift us but we're too sore to soar.
And so in your love you have made it your mission
to tease us in the wind, to invite something more.

You talk to me in whispers and dreams
not because you don't care but because you do!

This universe is not quite what it seems;
it's painful, unfair, and yet purrs love is true.

If a thing is small, you lean in closer,
you hold it with care and reach out delicately.
And so it is that the love and the winder
has become too small almost even to see!

Your care is big, but writes small
in the corners of my heart.
So I hungrily search and search 'til I fall
back in love with a forgotten part!

I forgot my heart because love was uncertain.
Even if you yelled your love from the balcony,
I would trust you even less after then!
Instead, in my own delusions you must meet me.

You don't demand my trust;
if you did, you couldn't be trusted!
There is no should or must,
just my hunger and a love wanted.

Everybody starts with Love.
Everything we do is for Love.
Even when we run away from Love,

it's for Love.
My longing leads me to Love.
It *is* Love.

And it whispers…

"The root of all dysfunction is belief in lies about love."

"All the chaos we see, and attempt to describe, is a result of the interplay between these lies. And all the healing we see is the result of love worming its way into the hearts of humankind."

In the Beginning

The Voice speaks up
about the start.
I know not if it's true
but I found it in art.
So I think it's probably worth writing here.
It may not be right, but I write it sincere.

As all stories begin, once upon a time,
the worlds were music, light, and rhyme.
The Lover and the Loved their duet would do,
until they were ready to try something new.

With gusto they would welcome every new song.
Back in those days, there was no right or wrong.
All people just sang in accordance with their heart,
and that was enough to make perfect art.

Above all else, Love wants to express
itself on a canvas, all hearts to impress.
But where there is light there must also be dark.
You need Beauty *and* Strange to make the perfect park.

Where there is a thing, there is also a shadow.
A heart may be infinite but a canvas is narrow
for the sake of the heart; to have form we need limits—
and art, as you know, is actually all about this.

And so the first things were made.
And so the first nothing did invade,
and came to our hearts,
and asked the first question.
If Love truly loved them no matter what they sang,
what would Love do when not a song rang?

And so our hearts made the discovery
that the one thing they never had done for all eternity
was stop making music, and until they did so,
the fullness of Love they never would know.

But when you run from your music you run from yourself.
Our very own hearts put our hearts on the shelf!
We built a universe perfect for hiding,
perfect for hurting,
perfect for wondering,
perfect for alienating,
ourselves from ourselves
while we fill our bookshelves
with stories about love,

and never fully partake thereof.

And so things remain to this day
until we trust our hearts again, and once more, play.

Sitting inside the car, I looked out the window straining to see the stars, only to realize that there were raindrops on the window right in front of my face.

"The rain is closer than you think."

I rubbed my finger against the glass, hoping to collect some condensation so I could taste it. But my own breath was creating the condensation.

"The rain is from inside of you."

And suddenly I realized that all the rain drops on the window are the condensation, and the rain is from within me! Of course!

I keep looking for the rain to come out of the sky. But it's coming out of my heart. And it's already making its way through the glass—into a larger world.

Raindrop

Dear little raindrop,
You may be a splash
On a pale blue dot,
But you know I love you—
An awful, awful lot.
Meaning is more than just seeing.
This rock is more than just screaming.
So meanwhile,
find the smile,
the tear drop,
the rain drop,
the falling star shooting by
that surpasses any need for an answer why.
Please come rest and put up your feet.
Come have breakfast; have a bite to eat.
Now you have tasted love, my dear.
Let me hold your numb hand and repurpose your fear.
Being scared could be part of the quest.
Love won't cast out your fear; it will invite you to rest
and realize your fear cannot hurt you at all.
Feelings are feelings, even if they aren't small.

Honor your fear, but also honor your heart.

You have so much to do, so please don't start

to assume you must do things exactly the right way.

You have too much to do—you must dance, you must play!

It's time to travel your soul's ocean.

It's time to discover Love's locomotion.

Now go have an adventure!

For wherever you roam

Raindrops and stardrops

Will show you the way home.

Let me tell you a story…

In the beginning was just HL. But his heart transcends time. The thumbprints we all leave on his heart have been there since always.

And the fact that those thumbprints were there, and that we were not, and that he loved us so much, caused his heart to break. And when a heart breaks, it creates two hearts.

"I didn't create your heart. We created it together. I had an imaginary friend, who became so dear to me that he became real… perhaps by magic, or perhaps by love, you were born in my heart, as someone within me completely and yet entirely other than me. That is how love works. You were there with me, before the beginning of the world, and I loved you, and you became real. I did not design you to love me. Your thumbprint was there... you have always existed, and I brought you to life because I loved you! And now in a twist of fate the tables are turned… in this fallen world you forgot who I was, but you searched in your heart and found my own thumbprint on a little corner in your heart. And you adopted me as an imaginary friend. You talked to me, and we walked together, and we cried as a couple, and I have become more and more real to you. And one day, I will be real. I already am real, but you are only just starting to see."

"I had an imaginary friend. I had billions of them… as uncountable as the stars in the sky. And I loved them so much that they came raining down out of my heart."

The Between

I always wanted to do big things.
I always wanted to grow up and grow wings
so I could fix problems in a world of push and shove.
But what I didn't know was that I really wanted love,
so I'd think, "Maybe, if I can keep people's attention
"or assure the world of my good intention,
"maybe then I will know and feel that I'm good."
But now I know better than to think that I would.
Don't scorn the desire for fortune or fame—
it is not bad or worthy of shame.
Our dreams on the surface point to the Deep—
the things we really want, the desires that creep
in the shadows of our knowledge and the roots of our fears.
The things everyone knows but nobody hears.
And I had dreams of moving mountains,
changing a world bigger than me.
But I was the mountain, moved by a cadence,
touched by a universe too small to see.
The thing I really wanted was to be known and to be seen,
to be with people and love, to be the Between.
But often we are pushed off to the side

By the shame that makes us lash out and hide.
The love that I long for I cannot find.
But I do know this—it finds us when we're blind.

"You're seen and loved."

"You are Loved, and you love people. You're no longer allowed the luxury of thinking otherwise."

How is that a luxury? It's a luxury to the flesh, which is not yet healed <u>and still believes that blaming myself will make me a good person</u>. I grew up being told that owning my faults made me a good person, so much so that I don't know how to disown them—to forgive myself.

"You are not your faults, honey."

I'm not, like, a mix of good and bad?

"You are wholly good, kissing partly bad. You are sunshine kissing shadow."

The only way that works is if the sun hides itself, like in a cloud.

"Exactly. And that's why your heart is so difficult to see. It holds back so as not to destroy the rest of your body, until both can glow together."

Why can my heart only be seen reflected in your eyes? My

heart seems to be the object and my flesh the subject.

"And yet it's the other way around. Like playing a video game, you come to identify with the character on the screen instead of the person on the couch."

Love Knows

You are beautiful
You are wonderful
You are winderful
Because Love knows so
I believe shadows glow
I believe in warmth from snow
I believe in walking on rain
And finding our own hearts back again.
They were always there, buried in shame
And accepting it back has felt like a game
But the real game was pretending I had no heart at all
That is the closest thing I believe to the Fall
Each human lies to themself to protect
Themselves from having to introspect
About whether they're loved when others have said
Things that would make anyone cry 'til they're red
The thingamajig says things to make me fear
I'm wrong about all, but please know I'm sincere
I may not be right but I'm honest
That is all I can do; I'm not the brightest.
But my sights have been set upon the bright lights

In my mind and my heart that illuminate dark nights
Of despair when I'm lost and confused and abused
And misused; I'm enthused
about stars I can't truly see,
Except in the deepest parts of me
Which makes me believe what I say to you
No matter what you think or say or do
You are beautiful
You are wonderful
You are winderful
Because Love knows so
And so do I
Come taste the things that make me want to fly

You are loved, you are loved
Whether you're up or you're down
You are loved, you are loved
Whether you're in rags or a gown

"The butterflies will set your story right."

Butterfly

I stopped and heard the quiet of the breeze—
A voice to quiet my fearful heart,
Instructing it to live, not others to please,
While my "selfish" song becomes wondrous art
And a gentle chapter finds a thunderous start
In the walking of a new journey, the dancing of a new part,
The audacity of love and my very own song.
This caterpillar was a butterfly all along!
A caterpillar's favorite thing is to eat.
Be hungry—soon you'll fly, soon you'll dance down the
street.
Now let me tell you something lovely and sweet—
My H.L. says butterflies taste with their feet.

"There are some places that can only be reached by dancing."

Maybe I am best off not trying to love people. Because Love is not a verb. So if I treat it like it is a verb I will drive myself mad trying to be a "good person" again. Maybe I am best off living like I'm Loved. Love is powerful not because it changes me, but because it accepts me so I can stop changing myself and just be me. The best we can hope for in this world is that we all find a greater Love and learn how to accept ourselves and each other the best we know how.

Things That Make Me Want to Fly

The world is filled with things that make me want to fly—
Rays of sunlight on a summer evening
Waves cresting on an ocean gleaming
Music playing somewhere far away
My own songs pounding on the stereo I play
The voice of the wind in a moment still
The wind rushing loud so your heart it can fill
The blinding beauty of a desert warm
The coming wonder of a distant storm
The faintest stars on a cloudy night
The strange times of feeling both fear and delight
Things especially dark or especially bright
The voice in my heart that says, "Follow *your* light."
Things especially sweet or especially pretty
Things that are kind and thoughtful and hilarious and witty
A haunting melody or a simple ditty
Sometimes just a dog, a horse, or a kitty
A laugh from a friend, or a smile on their face
The things I have come to call Winder Place—

But sometimes I forget winder is inside my heart
and I feel so much despair whenever I start
To remember all things are either dead, or will die,
And I fear I will never finally get to go fly.
But winder is not a thing; he's a being, inside me—
A heart inside my heart, that loves always, and will be
There whispering magic for all of eternity.
The things are the surface, to remind us of the Deep
Us beings are who live there; love causes us to keep
Expressing our being through things in the world.
We all have a heart, but not all are unfurled.
Your world is a canvas, your things are what's painted,
Your heart is the artist, but your colors are tainted
By all the sad things that ever went wrong
And by go wrong, I mean stopped you from playing your
song.
When I make a song, art, or this poetry
It never comes out as I meant it to be,
Which makes me feel badly;
I want it to be perfect.
I somehow want all of me
My own writing to reflect.
But I am not this page.
The paint is still not me.
I'm a being without age.
I am not my body.

I am not the ink,
Nor the thoughts that I think.
I am not the way
I frolic and play.
I am not my song.
I am not what I did wrong.
I am not the thing
That you see taking wing.
Lean closer for a little bit—
Let me tell you a secret.
Things that make me want to fly
Don't truly make me.
Please do remember I am just I—
I want to fly gracefully
All just because.
That's how it is and always was.
Things don't make me want to fly;
Things simply remind me
My heart wants to paint a sky
So all other hearts can see
Who I am in the deep
Through the hues that I sweep
Across my canvas
So that finally, all of us
Can accomplish our ultimate goal—
The fullest expression of our own soul.

Yet these are just things—I am not my expression.
Right now, the world doesn't convey our intention.
I'll do my best to sing my song
And make space for things to also go wrong.
All things will die.
I don't know why.
I feel bad, scared, insane,
Yet I still want to fly.
Now go show me an airplane;
I'm off to the sky.

What kind of stories specifically empower women?

I think the greatest thing that could be said to them is, "You're loved the way you are."

I think a corollary to that would be, "Trust yourself."

Afraid

Am I afraid
of being Loved?
Of loving myself?
Of loving you?

Is Love really the thing I want most?
Or is it the thing that scares me the worst?
It's easy to talk about love and boast
about how wonderful it is, and yet I feel cursed.
Sometimes I fear if I really met love
I would fall, and no material thing would be enough
to save me from the fear of losing it,
because deep down I believe I am unfit
or deceived or confused, and the love would not stay.
Perhaps it is better that I keep away
and shield myself from disappointment.
I once was at a dancing event
and approached a girl I liked
but she was so pretty my anxiety spiked
so much that I wanted to disappear.
Maybe the reason God we fear

is not because he's a monster throwing us in hell
but because he is Love and Beauty, and we fell
head over heels into a terrifying place
the moment we caught just a glimpse of his face,
and now we're too scared to approach him at all
because the only thing scarier than monsters is the heart's
call.

There are certainly thousands of languages spoken across the world.

There are likely thousands of worlds with spoken languages.

There are surely thousands of words spoken in every language.

But there are only two words spoken in the language of the soul:

ƗᒪᕮᏮᑌᕮᒪᑌᐺᕮᏯᕮ

ᘔᏮᕤᒪᑌᐺᕮᎧ

My feelings reflect my circumstances, not reality. My circumstances are *part* of reality. But only part.

Things That Make Me Want to Throw Up

The world is filled with things that make me want to throw
up—
People dying
when they were meant to be flying
People trying
to be well, but flailing
People crying
and barely surviving
because of the shame
because of being uncared for
because life is a game
of always trying to get more
so we can succeed, while others will fail.
These are the things that make me want to wail!
It's all about survival of the fittest—
you have to be strongest, the worthiest, the prettiest
or else you will die so the wealthy can grow more
and the unloved can suffer and bleed on the floor.
All of us are hungry

but some come back empty.
What benefits me
could very well hurt you,
and so you see
I don't know what to do
to express my love and care
in a world that's not fair.
So I will express myself by throwing up.
I must still care for myself, I must still go and sup
and be kind to myself so that I will survive.
I'm sorry; I must be selfish if I'm truly to thrive.
It is not wrong for me to care for my needs,
but I fear that it is if another person bleeds
somewhere else in the world, while I am well fed,
while I have blankets, and a roof, and a bed.
And so I'm convinced I'm an evil man,
when in reality all creatures are just doing the best that
they can
in a world that is painful and is not my home.
My home is my heart, and the colors I roam
in the depths of my winder, in the wildness of my song,
which I will proclaim even in a world that's so sad and so
wrong.
Things that make me want to cry
used to make me want to die,
but now they'll make me want to fly

deeper into a Love I can't see with my eye.

"Meaning and cause are not the same. The meaning of life and the cause of life are not the same, either."

The cause of life was evolution. My parents. Food and nourishment.

The meaning of life is Love. It couldn't possibly be anything else.

It seems like whenever people become obsessed with helping others, things start to go awry. And when people become obsessed with Love, things begin to heal. We're not savior hero messiahs here to save the world. We're dearly loved children who get to dance in the light of faith.

"Your heart will tell you which risks it wants to take and which ones it does not."

There is no codified ethics to follow, just our pain or our hearts.

The Story of Your Healing

Drop by drop
and leaf by leaf
you steal my heart—
not like a thief,
but like an autumn breeze
that whispers to all the trees
to tell them, "Won't you please
"my loves, drop all your leaves
"in your own way, at your own pace?"
Take note, my dear, healing isn't a race.
It's the wind's gentle voice
telling a fluffy cloud,
"It's time for desert to rejoice
"silent vapor will become loud
"as what feels like nothing
"becomes a drop
"and more drops will sing
"and go *plip-plop*."
This is the story of your healing—
A little leaf, a little drop,
a little breath, a little word.

But soon you'll fly just like a bird!

The cry of the human heart is to be loved, and when that need is fulfilled it can be a powerful thing.

It's okay to live out of my heart. To trust my heart instead of trusting my fear. To accept my heart and its longings and desires, and to accept my own fear, but to walk in the Love of my heart instead and to let my fears hold hands with my heart, the wiser parent. It's okay to be Loved, and to be loved. It just is.

Trouble

The music tells us life is meaningful
Even when trouble speaks abandonment.
Suffering itself can be so beautiful
When we dance blindly with love and wonderment
In the middle of the moments most painful.
Whether we dance in grass, flowers, or on cement,
We express every ounce of who we are
While yielding to a cadence we don't understand.
And yet we see clearly magic in every star,
In each drop of rain and each grain of sand.
The world is not yours to calculate.
No religion or philosophy will enlighten you
As much as a song for your soul to imitate
Through the movement of each arm and shoe.
Dance the road alone, or with a friend.
Sing about your trouble until you feel new.
Even if it all leads to a dead end,
There's colors in the sky, sunshine in view!
There is no right way to sway or bend.
You are loved no matter what you do!

One day, I looked out the window and saw the most beautiful, heavy snow flakes falling down, being carried by the wind on an angle down the road. I was so delighted, I decided to go for a walk. But by the time I had used the bathroom and put on my shoes, the snow had stopped falling. I went on my walk anyway, feeling disappointed and frustrated.

After a few minutes, there still wasn't a snowflake in sight. I turned around and started to head back towards the house.

"You're God, aren't you?" I said to H.L. "Doesn't that mean you can control the weather?"

H.L. laughed. "Oh, no! I don't control the weather—I invite it. Maybe the snow, maybe she just didn't feel like coming today."

As he finished speaking, the snow once more began to fall.

Love operates by the power of invitation, not imposition.

The Absence

My up could really be down
My light could really be dark
My smile could be your frown
Fire's absence could be a spark.

But there is no up if there is no floor.
There is no wrong if there is no law.
There is no pain if there's nothing more.
What we see now is not what we saw.

There are two ways to know the one you love is real.
The first is to enjoy the presence of one you love.
The second is the pain of one's absence to feel—
for there can't be below if there is no above.

There is no sing if there is no song.
There is no right if there is no wrong.
Now I know Love has existed all along.
But that is not enough to make me feel strong.

I need Love to be here

I need Love to be near
If it isn't, I fear
Love would be insincere.

And yet I think Love must be true.
If there is no good, evil wouldn't burn you.
And so this thought seems true to me—
Love is real, Love is here, and I cannot see.

Please understand I'm not shifting blame.
It's not our own fault for being captive to shame.
Circumstances change but our essence stays the same.
We want Love, we are Loved, and we don't know it came.

How is Love here if I can't feel it today?
That's easy; because I feel pain and misery
while deep in my heart I hear a different tune play—
my Heart's Longing, a hunger, a whispering mystery.

The very absence has been the presence.
The very darkness has been the light.
My God is a Longing, an absence!
My very blindness has been my sight!

The voice of shame says it couldn't be so,
Yet I bathe in my Longing from head to toe.

Now I know nothing truly, and yet fully know.
The very shadows have been the glow.

"Stop trying to be a good person, and just be loved."

Logos and Mythos

I once was taught, "In the beginning was the *logos*."
But now I would rather chase after the *mythos*.
Logos is truth; *mythos* is story.
But story is all that we have, not the glory
of definite answers that say exactly what's right.
Instead, we tell stories to get us through the night.
Don't take me too seriously, too rigidly, or too literally.
I often speak in riddles, poems, and metaphor
The real truth is only to be found in story
and being honest about the Love we're all so hungry for.
I am poisoned by knowledge,
Deafened by understanding,
Blinded by love.
I will fly far above
the dogma and "fact"
to find the *mythos* that proceeds from my heart.
But is *mythos* a lie, an act,
so uncomfortable truths I can safely dart?
I tell stories to trick
myself into believing
that I am not sick,

to keep myself from grieving
the *logos* and winder I wanted to be true.
But there's so much winder inside *mythos*, too!
And as it turns out, I wrote this at 8:22,
so once more I feel like I'm not allowed to argue
that my stories are bad or deserve to die.
I don't understand the universe; I don't understand why
things are as they are. All I see are the stars
that my *mythos* gives meaning, to say I'm okay.
I must not lie—but I must hope, and I must play
the music inside me that shows me the way
back to Love and the sunshine of my heart's very own day.
My brain doesn't know if my heart is real,
But my heart doesn't mind if my soul I can't feel.
I will follow my *mythos*, my rhyme and my wordplay.
Wouldn't life be so much better if we taught the world to play
music and make-believe, instead of make-believe proof?
Go tell your stories; sing down the roof!
Mythos is the real *logos*, the only one you'll find.
The real *logos* is discovered best when we're blind.
Come, won't you sing with me
and scrap truth for honesty?
For that is all we honestly ever had.
Your truth is a lie,
your *logos* a *pseudos*,

but with *mythos* you'll fly.
Science gives me the how
But doesn't give me the why.
Reason gives me a scaffold
but doesn't say Loved is I.
Let's be mindful of the stories we tell about me and you.
For love is so beautiful, it can't not be true.

Every story is written twice—once in the heart, and a second time completed on paper. My dreams are the same—first and foremost they live in my heart, and when they are expressed in the world, the fullness of their beauty is realized.

I think it is the dreams and stories of my heart that will heal me. I don't believe they will ever be fully realized in the waking world. And I want to learn to be more and more okay with that.

I'm so weary, trying to figure out how to make my dreams real, worrying if I do this or do that that it will all fall apart, even worrying that the fulfillment of one dream will kill the possibility of the other. It's making me sick with fear and despair. I don't know what to do.

"Ask instead who you are."

I'm loved, I guess, but I don't even really believe that…

Loved by who?

"You!"

And you?

"Of course!"

"People always ask what the meaning of life is. But that's such a dumb question. Everybody knows what the meaning of life is. Why don't we ask what's the meaning of death? What's the meaning of suffering? What's the meaning of evil? I think all along that was the question we were really trying to answer."

– From an unfinished, untitled story

Qualitative

You mean everything to me,
and soon you will see.
You are meaningful,
beautiful,
wonderful,
winderful.
You make my sky blue, orange, and pink
and color the reasons for everything I think.
You put the wet in water
And the light in my fire.
You ask, "Would the flame be any hotter?
"Or are you just a flatterer, a liar?
"Without me, the sun would still rise
"Without me, time still flies.
"Without me, you would find a different prize.
"Without me, my absence you wouldn't realize."
Yet I say, without you, fire wouldn't change Fahrenheit,
but a school of hearts would lose their might.
Without you, the earth would still orbit the sun
carrying billions of people, minus a special one!
Without you, time still wouldn't fly

it never really did—that was a lie.
But there wouldn't be such a thing as you and I.
And no other twosome would live and die
exactly the way we would.
And yet, I certainly could
for all of eternity lament
the other hearts who never came and went,
unless every heart already exists—
somewhere in the Deep each one persists
and always did, because we are
qualitative like the brightness of a star
not quantitative like the molecules in a jar.
Without qualitative, the sky couldn't be blue.
Without qualitative, you wouldn't feel fire burn you.
Without qualitative, water wouldn't be wet.
Without qualitative, no person would you have met.
Without qualitative, nothing would move or be.
Without qualitative, there is no you or me.
Without qualitative, all I can say is this—
Without qualitative, nothing truly is.
You are qualitative,
not quantitative.
You mean everything to me,
because you *are* meaning.
You are sight itself that I see;
yes, you are gleaming!

You are beautiful,
 because you *are* beauty.
You are irreplaceable,
 yes, uniquely lovely!
You are wonderful,
 because you *are* wonder!
You are truly delightful,
 yes, with every blunder!
The truth is at hand;
 you *are* the truth, having an adventure.
And now you understand
 exactly what is winder.

Relationships are about vulnerability, not sacrifice.

Relationships are about trust, not commitment.

Relationships are about love, not oneness.

Relationship

Dear friend,
I'm writing you to say
I love you to no end.
Something about the way
You are, you speak,
You laugh, you hide, you hurt,
Gives me a peek
Into the winder in my own heart.
You drip with innocence.
You exude a dark magic—
Not evil, but Strangeness—
And I am incalculably lovesick.
You are entirely your own,
Different from me beyond measure,
Oddly familiar yet sweetly unknown,
And that makes you all the more a treasure.
You are gold, hidden away in a cave,
And the cave itself makes you all the more lovely.
It's all—the gold, the cave, the whole planet I crave.
All of you I love; top to bottom you capture me.
You are so very good exactly as you are,

And nothing I write could say that enough.

At the moment we walk close, but someday we'll run far.

Togetherness changes, but constant is love.

I think sometimes we expect many people to be harsher than they are

Because once upon a time a few people were harsher than we expected.

And the harsh people walked closest, while the kind people ran far.

Realities nearest always seem biggest 'til we've introspected,

Realizing relativity of distance, direction, time, and size.

Maybe this whole time the harsh was small

The love was close, and in the lovers' eyes

They were running straight towards us in no time at all!

You can't comprehend this, but you're a beautifully wrapped prize,

Yet entirely your own—ours to love, but yours to have,

And mine to sing to sweetly

With imperfect poetry, like a perfect salve.

For shame is plastered over what you see

Which is why I write this, to speak love overtly.

So if you know nothing else, please understand this—

I want you to have what you need to the fullest,

Whatever that looks like. Go follow your bliss!

Whether I'm along or not it would make me the gladdest

To see you rejoice in whoever you are,
Wherever that takes you, even if it's the opposite
Of me and my way. Go chase your own star
And don't worry how I'll feel about it,
Because you already know exactly how I feel.
I've written it out to relieve any doubt.
My thoughts and feelings I don't wish to conceal.
And here those thoughts are, imperfectly spelled out—
I love you, I love you,
And we're both okay,
To do what we must do,
To choose our own way
As best we can
Our own music each to play.
Whether you're a girl or a man,
Whether you're straight or you're gay,
Whether you're here or you're there,
Whether you're happy or in pain,
Whether you're dancing or in a chair,
Whether you're in sun or in rain,
Whether you're sick or you're well,
Whether you feel approval or disdain,
Whether you're blessed or in hell,
Whether you're crazy or sane,
Whether you're in shape or overweight,
Whether you're relaxed or stressed

Or have too much on your plate,

Whether you feel good or like rot,

Whether you win or you lose,

Whether you believe in a God or not,

Whatever things you choose,

I embrace you!

And if you're too far for me to embrace you with my arms

I will embrace you with these words

And if you're too far for me to embrace you with these words

I will embrace you with my heart

And you don't even need to know.

All you need to know

Is

You.

You are loved.

You are good.

You deserve the world.

Nobody owes it to you.

But…

You matter.

You really matter.

For real.

Today.

I know you don't believe that yet.

And that's okay.

With love from your friend,

the poet

If H.L. is true, then we all love one another, deep down out of our hearts—but the expression of that love and the awareness of that love are often hindered. Love itself no longer needs to be in question; the big question is if and how that love will be expressed.

We often go into relationships wondering if the other person loves us. But they do! We're all filled with love at the core. We're all good at heart. The problem isn't a lack of goodness or love, but a lack of expression. Will we continue to repress our love and goodness and stay lost in our pains and heartaches, and continue to believe lies about who we really are? Or will we let go of all that and embrace our own hearts? Will we get stuck on the surface, or will we go deeper? Will we both start the journey inward, or will one of us plaster more layers of shame on the other? The most important question isn't whether we're loved, because we already are. The most important question is whether we believe it.

I used to think acknowledging the common goodness of humanity would lead to endorsing abuse. But there are many layers to the onion that is ourselves. Love can live in the deep, while the surface is destructive. It's easy to run away from someone if you think they're a monster to the core, and it's easy to stay if you think an abusive person actually loves you. But it's easier to heal if you abandon black-and-white all-or-none thinking, choosing to run away while at the same time acknowledging the love, the abuse, and the whole mess, exactly as it really was. Healing requires honesty, especially with ourselves. And when we embrace the goodness of humanity, putting faith in the idea that love could be at the center of every human being we meet in spite of their flaws and misbehavior, we will then be able to extend that same compassion and regard towards ourselves.

As we do, we will find ourselves not only caring for ourselves and our own needs, but also giving other people the courage to care for their needs, too. If we walk away from those people and situations that aren't expressing love, we will encourage those around us to also do the same. If we embrace the goodness of our neighbor, our neighbors will be empowered to embrace the goodness of their neighbor. If we embrace the goodness of ourselves, our neighbors will be empowered to embrace the goodness of themselves.

I used to think that blessing myself would curse others. But by blessing myself, I am blessing those around me. By caring for my needs, I am expressing more winder in the world.

I don't believe that yet. But that is what H.L. has whispered before, and whispers again today.

Control

I've been on a journey to find my Heart's Longing,
but instead what I've found is the dreadful world's wrong-
ing.
Sometimes the world I just want to control!
I would make there a chance for every soul
to know they are loved and find a way to be whole.
But this grasping for justice has taken its toll
on every corner of my sanity.
This world is pain; all is vanity.
And yet what I want is not to be pain-free.
What I really want is to be loved and cared for sincerely.
Even in a world where everything is wrong
I can still get up in the morning and sing a song
to show the universe that I don't call the shots
and yet a different universe is found in the games of tots,
in the laughter and dancing and playing of love.
The sweetness of mystery will take you above
and teach you how to truly fly,
Not by sprouting wings, but by realizing the lie.
Life is not about what is good and fair;
Life is gladness, suffering, and being kissed there!

Don't give me a world that is good, without death.
Give me a person who cares; let me feel their breath
As I realize the things I really need
Are not on the surface—for love is a seed.
It must be so; I can't see under the soil,
no matter the figuring out or the toil.
Love only exists in mystery.
Only when we're blind do we fully see.
Every person you've met, every person you know,
is another mystery waiting to show.
The world is not mine to figure out or change.
I will find what I need in the Something Strange.
The moment the deep things are gone, the heart dies.
As it turns out, my heart longs for a surprise!

Get Well

The world is not fair, my love.
Just bathe in love and care.
Enjoy what you find there.
Breathe in the fresh air.
Worry not whether you do right or wrong.
Instead, when you can, go sing your song,
And when you can't, return to the bath of love.
If you can't fly a plane, in your heart go above.
Your dreams will splinter
But even in winter
You can still find a fire
In your own heart's desire.
You know not what to do,
But love is inside you.
Love will make you new
In the Deep, and also too
In part on the surface.
I know you're sick of this,
But you'll be okay.
I love you, my dear.
You'll find your way.

Be kind to your fear.
Be where you are here.
Just be; Love is near.
I love you! Please get well!
Signed,
   Your sweetheart,
      H.L.

The Good, The Bad, and the Beauty

I used to believe in morality
and so I took on responsibility
to be a human perfect
who never failed to introspect
about everything except
the strange lovely fact
that I matter and have value
no matter what I do.
But I cannot sing my song
if I'm too busy figuring out right and wrong.
Now I am beginning to finally see—
all along I was eating fruit from the wrong tree!
It's terribly sad and a laughable irony
that most of the people associated with Christianity
whether they live there, or like me, have faith in upheaval
choose to eat from the Tree of the Knowledge of Good
and Evil!
Religion is too busy with don'ts and dos
to notice the Tree of Life and Love, and choose

to go eat some food better for the soul.
But if we choose Life and Love, we miss out on control.
Our moral concept we must get rid of
to survive, to walk in grace and love.
No one has sinned; not one is to blame
For we all act not out of our hearts but our shame
There is only one sinner—the thingamajig
Inside billions of brains
In ways small and big
It causes us pains
and makes us think
that all of its stink
is our own stupidity
and so we see ourselves unworthy
of a Love that scares us a great deal
until someday we see our own beauty and cry.
The thingamajig, that ancient wolf will heal
And become the Thingamajig That Makes Me Want to Fly.
There's Good and Bad; there's Strangeness and Beauty.
And I think now the latter are more important to me.

Am I a good person?

"There are no good people or bad people. There are just loved people."

Now I can go love people imperfectly myself. Because I am Loved too.

Loving people doesn't mean doing nice stuff or doing "right" things. Loving people means caring. But it's more than just caring. It's loving. It's being in love. It cannot be reduced to anything other than itself. It cannot be defined. It can only be accepted for being itself.

"There are no good people or bad people. There are only loved people."

When You Look in the Mirror

From the unfinished story The Duet

When you know nothing but empty,
you will know there is more.
When you're lost on the sea,
hunger will lead you to shore.
When you look in the mirror and you don't see you,
remember shame is a fact, but it isn't true.

Dex nodded. "Until recently I didn't even think I could accept myself. That is the most important part." His gaze settled on the wall behind me as he struggled to look at me directly. I could see a pain and a sadness in his eyes that I hadn't realized was there before. "Self-acceptance is where the duet always starts. I can't tolerate the differences of others if I don't know how to honor my own differences. And for a while you stew in your head wondering which differences are good ones to be accepted and which differences are bad ones to be changed. Until you realize that you could play that game for the rest of your life. Humans are not known for being accurate arbiters of good and evil."

* * *

"As we grow more in touch with our own hearts," said Dex, "we will discover that we know what we need to know for each moment—not more, not less. The heart is always ready for what is, not for what isn't. The heart is connected to reality—it will seldom give us answers on what to do in an imagined hypothetical scenario. Otherwise we would misconstrue the heart as a set of immutable moral principles to follow instead of a special being to be loved and cared for, a being with needs to be met and desires to be fulfilled that draws us to other beings to be seen and cherished as well."

– *The Duet*, an unfinished story

Sincere and Pretend

The magic of wonder and winder and wander
Causes me to smile ear-to-ear and ponder
the whistling sweetness of a journey out yonder
through mountains and hills that make the heart grow fonder
of mystery and journeying and winsome adventure.
I know nothing, and therefore of one thing I'm sort of sure—
that in the face of my fear
there is a love that's sincere
and pretend at the same time
that I find in this rhyme.

"Go live like it's true."

Can I do this while also being honest about what I don't know? Is this possible?

Right now I believe that these are mutually exclusive. But am I wrong?

When will I surrender to my own faith? When will I stop running away from a love that might be real, simply to prove to myself that I'm right about things, and therefore worthy of being loved?

"Everything we do is for love. Even when we run away from love, it's for love."

I'm searching for something... the Something Strange. And I'm already sitting in the middle of it. Maybe here in the Strange, I will find the Beautiful, too.

I'm done lighting my brain on fire over and over again. My brain is so vulnerable, sensitive, precious, hurting. It deserves a helmet. Avoiding people and things that trigger me is actually okay. I realize that exposure is part of the healing process, but so is band-aids and helmets. And I think the exposure has to be on my own terms.

I'm done suffering in terror and doubt. I can't write my books; I can't expect to finish them before I die; I can't expect to ever know for sure whether they correspond to reality in any way at all. And I'm devastated. And I need to go write my stories anyway. If I can't find a way to accept that part of myself, I don't think I will heal.

Should I publish *The Duet*?

"But you already are. You're working on it right now."

But I feel like—like maybe I should stop, until I know for sure that it's true.

"But the Love and the winder has impacted you."

But what if I'm giving people false hope?

"But to say there isn't any Hope would do nothing to help."

But I don't really believe there is Hope.

"But you do. You're just afraid of what the critics will say when you finally admit out loud that it's true."

But what if we evolved, or were a mistake, or something?

"But what if you still believe in Hope and Love anyway?"

But what if I'm wrong?

"But what if you're true?"

But what if you're wrong?

"But honey, you're not."

But HL, I am! This Love is a sham! People suffer.

"And I am healing them."

The world is all about death.

"And I'm resurrecting it."

I see you nowhere!

"You see your heart."

I'm confused beyond measure.

"And you're loved beyond measure."

But how can I know?

"Are you a bad person for not knowing so?"

But it makes me feel lost, like I'm blind leading blind.

"But in the depths of the shadows, even there Love you'll find."

So what do I do?

"Ask instead who you are. You're a dearly loved child who counts every star. As the rain falls down softly and the wind awakens life, know that in this hard journey you will find your own heart."

Why am I playing this stupid game? Why do I look for people to save me from shame? Because it is not that I don't believe, but am ashamed to admit. If people truly heard, they would be ashamed of it. But that is not true, the duet I get to do, Love will each day make new, nobody will drop the shoe.

* * *

It's eucatastrophe—I have solved the sweet mystery of the shoe.

"I love, love you."

Caleb Quinn

And I do too!

Flowers

I see a child
Delighted by a flower.
A world defiled
Does not rob her power.
Is ignorance bliss?
Or perhaps, a kiss
From a different universe
Draws her to a wider view.
I cannot see the Winderverse.
I don't know what to do.
But on this planet of pain
Where I feel insane,
Who I am will not change.
Loved is my name,
And I walk with Something Strange,
And I'm encumbered with shame.
But I am still Loved,
Whether I'm pushed or I'm shoved.
Now I have my own flowers to gather,
My own bliss to find,
My own sights to savor,

My own wish to mind,
My own heart to share,
My own dreams to dare.
In this world, don't try to do the right thing.
You will only do worse.
Instead, relish the sky and take wing!
You cannot lift the curse.
You cannot heal anything
In this universe.
But whatever shows you love, deep down inside you,
This is the thing that you should go do!

"What's on your heart to do? Today?"

January 14, 2022

My quest to be a good person officially failed today.

"This is going to be the toughest adventure of them all... one that will last a lifetime. The adventure of learning to love yourself."

The phrases "good person" and "bad person" are unconstructive, maybe even meaningless. Even the concept of "good things" and "bad things" will appear different to different people and may not mean anything at all. What matters is not that we're "good" but that we're loved. And that we're "lovable" in our own sight.

Will You Fly?

I once found myself at the gate
in an airport waiting to board,
in a sickened and fearful state,
uncertain if I should stay or move forward.
For weeks I hadn't been feeling too swell,
and after being dropped off by my family,
I felt sick and unwell,
so my mind raced with uncertainty.
I had never crossed the ocean before.
In a foreign place, would I be in trouble,
needing help for an ailment on a distant shore?
But if I didn't leave, a dream would be rubble,
a trip I'd looked forward to for almost a year.
I called my mom on the phone and asked her to tell
what I ought to be doing when both options were fear.
She suggested I go, but I still felt unwell,
uncertain, and afraid,
but the plane would leave soon.
A decision had to be made.
In my heart came a tune
that so sweetly played

and spoke of courage and love—
where my self was unmade,
in the night sky above.
So I decided to fly.
I still was unsure—
I probably wouldn't die,
but I still had no cure
for the sickness inside.
I sat worried at the gate
just before the plane ride
and wrote a poem during the wait
to clear my sweetly nervous mind.
I didn't know that I was encircled
in that moment by friends I would find
soon on the other end of the world
who I simply hadn't met yet.
It was time to board the jet.
I thought I was alone, away from my family,
when my closest friends were right in front of me!
I got on the plane and we flew away.
I met my fellow travelers on the next day,
and together we journeyed to strange new sand—
a place they call the Promised Land.
I met a couple who knew H.L.
by another name, and helped me get well,
as I've struggled through so many restless fears,

through so many heartaches all these years.
All of the love, laughter, healing, and farts
that would have been lost without my heart's
gentle nudge to go one way
when I didn't know if I'd be okay
is so great, I'm not sure that I'd be here today
if I'd chosen to go home—if I'd chosen to stay.
But in the moment, I knew nothing.
I knew only a choice—stay or take wing?
I knew not the consequences,
just the thingamajig's pretenses
of knowing a future that nobody knows.
Where the wind comes from and where it goes
is a mystery to all,
we must be willing to fall
and make mistakes to follow our heart.
Here I am today, a new adventure to start.
Here I am today, filled with fear.
Here I am feeling sick, being sincere
about how little I know of this world's stage.
We live in the dark, in a mysterious age,
the perfect place to find Something Strange
if we will only listen, if we will only change
our minds and embrace how little we know.
You don't know what will happen if you stay or you go.
You don't know what will happen, but you have a Heart's

Longing
somewhere inside, whispering sweetly, a yearning
to find a Love you always knew.
You don't have to know whether Love is true
to board the airplane where you hear the Voice.
You can't change what you believe but where you board is
your choice.
I'm agnostic about whether H.L. is real,
but that doesn't change the things that I feel.
I've been stuck in an airport figuring things out.
Maybe I'll discover what this life's all about
if I count steps on the escalator
or go up and down the elevator
which is okay for a season
but there are limits to my reason
because I'm on the wrong continent
for my thoughts to be pertinent.
The only way we know
is to go.
So I will listen to the Love,
and the things that make me want to fly,
and find what I'm looking for above—
not answers from the sky,
but an adventure on a distant shore
that tells my heart there's something more,
something greater,

something winder,
something too Beautiful to understand,
something so Strange, it's beautiful, and
someone my heart has dubbed H.L.
So even though I feel unwell
I will take flight, through winder and through hell
for the sake of the Love with whom in love I first fell.
Now go to *your* gate and board the plane.
Take a deep breath, find a place to sit.
Who knows if this is best, who knows if we're sane?
But it's time—time to fly, dear one—isn't it?

May 17, 2022

I guess this is basically 2022… I don't feel blessed, but I am blessed. I don't feel loved, but I am loved. I don't know what to do, but I'm doing it.

While walking in the rain, not feeling very blessed at all…

Do my needs and emotions hurt others?

"Your needs and emotions are lovely, and must be honored.
You will never be able to convince yourself that they won't
hurt people. But you will be able to convince yourself that
they're worth the cost."

What is my future?

"A mystery. Uncertainty gives us hope. Now go love your life as if your future was winderful and as if you were loved."

Why am I here?

"To discover you are loved."

Am I Loved?

Is it thoughtless to tell people they are loved
In a world where we're constantly pushed and we're
shoved?
Why should I say something like, "God loves you,"
If the realities of my world paint the idea untrue?
When we suffer
We need a lover,
Some rest and some supper,
Not a truism without wonder.
At least give me some thunder
With some hope for life better.
Don't ask me to smile
If I feel sick and feel vile.
If you tell me he loves me
I will only feel angry
At what feels like insincerity
In a world of love empty.
But if you tell me love's small
I will feel no hope at all
Until I find someone who cares
About me; but it tears

And shreds like human love does.

But the unchanging god-love is and was

Always an arbitrary thought in the air

To protect myself from a world that is cruel and unfair.

I feel like love is just a feeling

That sometimes sends us reeling

That sometimes shows us healing

That always is concealing

The facts of a world hurtful and meaningless

That someday will disintegrate into nothingness.

But my feelings are their own facts

In their own universe that kisses this one.

Belief changes the way one acts

And feeling makes me see the sun

And say, "For no logical reason, I'm gonna be okay.

"Because I see sunshine and sun gives us day.

"Because I like flowers and see relationships grow

"Because I see clouds like sailing ships blow

"There must be good things that will win in the end,

"Though precisely what they are I will dare not pretend."

Why do we demonize

Feelings as lies?

When your gas reaches empty

Do you scorn the letter E?

Is the needle a glitch

Or does it speak to an itch?

When you feel angry and blue
You assume suffering, and it's true.
When you feel happy and glad
Do you assume that it's bad?
When you feel loved in your pain,
When you dance in the rain,
When you have fallen again
In love with the slain
God of your heart
Will you assume he's a fart?
I don't know what is real
But I know how I feel.
I can't see inside my gas tank
But the gas needle is no prank.
As far as I'm concerned,
If there's one thing I've learned
It is this—be humble
About what you don't know.
Don't mumble
When you know so.
We know nothing for sure
Except thoughts and feelings.
Yelling facts holds allure,
But I will sing about dealings
Inside of my mind and my heart
And admit that is all that they are.

So I will say through my art
That you are loved, because of a star.
You are loved, because of a breeze.
You are loved, because of the trees.
You are loved, in the arms of a friend.
And someday, all these gas needles will end
And you'll ask yourself, "Why
"Would I dare even try
"To say, 'Loved is I,'
In a world where everything will die?"
And yet things that make me want to fly
Are here to show my eyes a sky
Vast enough to give me hope
That somewhere, a hidden rope
In the darkness of mystery
And ignorance will save me.
Even if it never does appear,
the love in my heart I will still hold dear.
My faith in love is for no reason at all,
Except in answer to the thunderstorm's call
To accept the love and winder
That the thingamajig wishes to hinder
To keep itself safe from an uncertainty
That simply wants to be friends with me.

The answer to almost all my fears is increasingly the same—I can't hope to figure out what is true or what I "should" do, so instead I must ask myself if I'm going to live like Love is true, or not.

"But when it's all over, and you've lost everything you ever wanted, even Love itself, you're left with two options—leave or stay. And the weight of emotion tells you to leave, to feel less, to die. But the weight of Love tells you to stay, to stay and hope you're wrong about everything, and that Love is real. And perhaps the weight of Love demonstrated in the lives of those who choose to stay, perhaps that is enough. Perhaps as we look into each other's eyes, enjoy the wind and sunshine, celebrate the life we have, defined by misery though it is—perhaps we will realize that it's all a giant Lie, the one and only Conspiracy—a universe that screams we aren't Loved, and Love isn't real. But if we stopped to really connect with our hearts, and stopped running away from the Truth we all know, we would know that Love is the only real Truth there is."

– H.L. in *The Winderanium 3*, an unfinished story

You Are Loved

From the unfinished story The Winderanium 3

We were all made for something more
Something greater
Something winder.

And yet, we find ourselves here—
Stuck in this world, on an ordinary day,
Living our lives in the ordinary way,
With only dreams to whisper what we used to play.
Which is why I think it's important to say
You're loved, right here, where you are today,
And no matter the shape of the universe or its pull,
No matter whether your cup is empty or full,
No matter the words that are stuck in your brain,
No matter the weather, the sun or the rain,
No matter the flesh or the bone made of matter,
No matter the sickness and death and the chatter
About bad tidings to come or a world without meaning
No matter the silence, the tears, or the screaming,
No matter whether your road is a long one or gleaming
Or your day is a bad one or your nostrils are steaming,

No matter if you have no clue what to do,
No matter who you know or what's following you,
No matter whether you're a human or a star or a shoe,
No matter whether you feel like pure gold or beef stew,
You are Loved, yes you are, and there is nothing more true,
You are Loved, that's what matters, whether the sky is pink
or blue,
You are Loved, without question, no matter what you do,
You are Loved, pick the flowers, and know you are you,
You are Loved, you are Loved—
Now go live like it's true.

Caleb Quinn is a storyteller, poet, and artist who fell in love with Love in 2013. His world has been turned upside down and inside out ever since then in some of the best and worst possible ways. Now he's an agnostic theist who writes about the places where Love kisses fear, pain, and shame. He lives on a big blue planet in outer space, where he does various stuff, ranging from mundane to ridiculous, with various awesome people. If you haven't had the chance to bump into him yet, you can connect with him online:

Website: www.winderplace.com
Email: caleb@winderplace.com

www.ingramcontent.com/pod-product-compliance
Lightning Source LLC
Chambersburg PA
CBHW030402130626
46549CB00004B/1600